SUNITI NAMJOSHI

The Artful Transgressor

Writers of the Indian Diaspora

SUNITI NAMJOSHI
The Artful Transgressor

C. VIJAYASREE

Series Editor
Jasbir Jain

RAWAT PUBLICATIONS
Jaipur and New Delhi

ISBN 81-7033-678-3

Published by
Prem Rawat for *Rawat Publications*
Satyam Apts., Sector 3, Jain Temple Road, Jawahar Nagar, Jaipur - 4 (India)
Phone: 0141 651748 / 657006 Fax: 0141 651748
e-mail : rawatbooks@pinkline.net

Delhi Office
G-4, 4832/24, Ansari Road, Daryaganj, New Delhi 110 002
Phone: 011-3263290

Typeset by Rawat Computers, Jaipur
Printed at Nice Printing Press, New Delhi

In memory of
my brother ***Karunakar***
&
his wife ***Adilakshmi***
who gave me parental love and affection

Contents

Series Editor's Preface

It is a pleasure to be introducing another volume on the writers of the Indian diaspora. As every new volume is completed we begin to see how tentative all definitions are and how they need to be deconstructed, opened out in different ways, before they can be put together in any relevant way.

Suniti Namjoshi has been active on the literary scene for more than three decades. She is mid-way of the fourth. During these years she has written both singly and in collaboration, in verse as well as in prose, fables and dystopias, fantasy and satire. And as she has travelled from genre to genre, she has also moved from country to country and tested herself against different cultural frameworks. Through this writing she has challenged both diasporic and feminist narratives of culture, and has resisted any singular anchorings.

Where do we place such a writer whose attitude to the past is neither nostalgic nor political, who critiques culture through universal paradigms and selects areas of universal discrimination for instance the categories of gender and class, for her themes; and who also positions the animal world against the human? A writer who wishes to move outside culture specifies even as she uses cultural myths, absorbs fairy tale narratives of an 'alien' culture and intermixes the idiom?

Do writers who challenge norms belong to tradition? Can we trace a tradition of the fabulous or of utopia and locate her. These and similar other questions are raked up. At once reminding one Borges and Marquez on the one hand, on the other she harks back to Rokeya Shakawat Hosain's "Sultana's Dream" and the Bhakti poets. At home in all cultures and alienated from all, the world is being shaped closer to the heart's desire in this rewriting of myths and intertextual narratives.

The multi-dimensional explorations which Professor Vijayasree has brought to her work enable us to relate to Namjoshi's work at several different levels as we move from the readerly to the writerly text.

Jasbir Jain

Acknowledgements

This book has taken long – almost three years – to emerge in its present form. During this period, Suniti Namjoshi pervaded my study, dining and cooking areas and in fact the entire living space in my home. I thank my family – my husband Ravichandra and my daughter Ujwala – for putting up and putting up with this house guest so heartily.

I am grateful to Sunitiji not only for her prompt responses to my persistent queries, but also for her creative work which afforded me a perfectly pleasurable experience.

I thank Professor Jasbir Jain, the General Editor of this series whose faith in me prompted me to undertake this challenging project.

C. Vijayasree

Preface

Suniti Namjoshi who began writing in the late sixties has been publishing consistently, and she has brought out several volumes of poems, fables and other works of fiction. The productivity alone does not make Namjoshi significant; rather the range, depth and variety of her work and the remarkable originality of thought earn her distinction. Namjoshi is an experimental writer who dares to tackle a variety of subjects; to employ a range of techniques and in so doing dares to risk failure. Much of her work is genuinely distinguished; taken in totality, it is incredibly rich and is an impressive testament to a life differently lived, an intellect sharp and capable of original perceptions, and a creative genius inventive and innovative. Namjoshi's is a substantial body of work deserving more recognition and critical attention than it has so far been accorded. There have been reviews and readings of single texts, occasional discussions of her work in books/articles devoted to the writings of the Indian diaspora, or to lesbian literature. I am aware of a couple of research dissertations on her work, but no full-length study of Namjoshi's work has yet been attempted. I consider myself fortunate to undertake this pleasant task of offering critical readings of all her major texts in this study.

My interest in Namjoshi's work began at least a decade and a half ago, when I presented a paper on her *Feminist Fables* at a national conference on Commonwealth Literature. The paper was received with much enthusiasm and this confirmed my own belief that Namjoshi was a writer worth serious critical attention. I kept steadily in touch with Namjoshi's subsequent work and included discussions of her work in my publications on the writings of the Indian diaspora. The present project began nearly three years ago when Professor Jasbir Jain had asked me to do a full length study of Suniti Namjoshi's work for a series on 'Writers of the Indian diaspora' she was editing for Rawat Publishers, Jaipur. The suggestion was more than welcome since the subject of study was close to my heart.

Once I began to re-read Namjoshi's work to write about it, the task proved to be much more difficult than what I had imagined it would be. The assignment turned out to be demanding for various reasons: Namjoshi's work is elusive and sprints buoyantly ahead of any attempt at paraphrase. Each reading of her layered texts brings out newer possibilities and one cannot rush into easy generalizations about her work. Secondly, her work is rich in allusions. She draws on Greek as well as Christian myths and legends, fables and fairy tales, old and new writers and weaves an intricate network of intertexts into her texts. Any attempt at an analysis of Namjoshi's work requires to grasp this interconnectedness and this can some times send one on an endless search for the missing links. Basically, when Namjoshi narrates her tale she does not serve the meaning on a platter to her readers; in fact she does not even believe that there is a single authoritarian meaning that a writer can dictate. Instead, she leaves it to her readers to draw their own inferences and arrive at their own decoding of the texts. Namjoshi texts reveal themselves in slow degrees, gradually and gratifyingly. A reader does not work on them; they work on the reader. This happened to me too. Each new book of Namjoshi would send me back to a re-reading of her earlier work and each reading revealed possibilities unearthed earlier. The whole enterprise has been an enjoyable and enriching experience. Knowing that I am risking overstatement and oversimplification, I have attempted to stake out a critical trail for others to follow or abandon, through the challenging and largely unchartered terrain of Namjoshi's work.

Feminist critics have identified acts of "revision, appropriation and subversion" as central to much of feminist writing. I use the term 'Transgression' to include all these as well as an urge to usher in transformation that eventually is the goal of all these acts of revolution. As the title of this book suggests, I have mainly focused on transgressional and transformational aspects of Namjoshi's themes as well as techniques. This, I believe, is an important clue to the understanding of Namjoshi's work.

Namjoshi represents the tensions of inhabiting and writing from margins and in-between spaces as a woman, as a lesbian and as a diasporic writer. She does not, however, show any anxiety about resolving the tensions emanating from such a complex and complicated subject position, but sophisticates the art of tapping the plural possibilities afforded by her positioning in a fluid state. Both in her life and art, she is a non-conformist; she transgresses norms of societal and literary conventions; stresses the need for looking at life from alternative perspectives so that the conventional hierarchies of class, race and gender get demolished and more acceptable and egalitarian perspectives may emerge. To her, writing eventually becomes a quest for charity, charity being the highest ideal of human life. Her writing -- poetry and fiction -- is art of struggle, formal and philosophical and has taken a variety of forms. She negotiates the contraries that mark her experience -- East and West, rich and poor, center and periphery and understands the play of these polarities as part of the dynamics of power. Her works often make a critical analysis of power politics and chart the impact of power on human life and societal relationships. I have, therefore, studied her work, particularly fictional work, primarily as stories of struggle that deal with relations of power.

Chapter I examines the personal and conceptual contexts of her work. The subsequent chapters trace the major developments in Namjoshi's thought and art in a rather sequential narrative demonstrating Namjoshi's increasing penchant for non-hegemonic forms of thought and expression which eventually culminates in the production of dialogic and conversational texts where in the reader is incorporated as a co-author. Chapter II looks at the first phase in her creative writing -- her early concerns, and her struggles with poetic form. Chapter III focuses on the radical changes that occurred in her personal life and the manifestation of these changes in her poetic work contained in anthologies – *The Jack Ass and the Lady* and *The Authentic Lie*, which I describe as the 'Conversion Poems'. Then I move on to the seminal phase in her writing, her radical retelling of fables in *Feminist Fables* and *From the Beside Book of Nightmares* and her serious preoccupation with re-visionist myth-making and show how Namjoshi texts turn subversive, volcanic and transformational. Namjoshi is meticulous to the minutest detail in matters of craft and it is fascinating to observe how she constantly strives to evolve more and more sophisticated forms of fictional and poetic expression. Chapter V is devoted to Namjoshi's use of feminist fabulation in *The Conversations of Cow* and *The Mothers of Mayadiip*. In the next chapter, I argue that Namjoshi's work acquires a playful tone in her later work and demonstrate how she plays with ideas, ideologies and identities in *The Blue Donkey Fables* and *Saint Suniti and the Dragon*. The seventh chapter is devoted to a discussion of her next work of fiction, *Building Babel* that creates a collaborative reader and leaves the narrative open ended so that each reader may add her/his own version to the text. I added a rather hesitant conclusion since any attempt at a neat summing up of Namjoshi's work goes against the spirit of her art and philosophy. I added a brief note on her latest work of fiction -- *Goja* -- as a postscript since this book arrived after the manuscript was dispatched to the publisher.

Finally, writing a book on a living writer of versatile talent who constantly explores new fictional territory has been an extremely enriching experience. I have not had to contend with imaginary conversations with writers of bygone days, but could hold an online dialogue with the subject of my study. Namjoshi was kind enough to respond to my queries and give me clarifications whenever I sought her help. These conversations are presented in the appendix so that the reader of my book will have the benefit of getting to know the tale as well as the teller. However, I wish to stress that I alone am responsible for the critical views put forth in this study.

C. Vijayasree
Osmania University
Hyderabad

List of Abbreviations

AL	*The Authentic Lie*
BB	*Building Babel*
BF	*The Blue Donkey Fables*
CC	*The Conversations of Cow*
CP	*Cyclone in Pakistan*
FBB	*From the Bedside Book of Nightmares*
FF	*Feminist Fables*
JL	*The Jackass and the Lady*
MM	*The Mothers of Maya Diip*
MP	*More Poems*
P	*Poems*
SS	*Saint Suniti & The Dragon*

1

Texts and Contexts

> The house made of candy, the witch wicked; but now that they are outcasts and must live in the forest, to whom can they turn? Gretel takes charge. She is braver and wiser. Besides it is distinctly possible that in this wild witch's world she stands a better chance. She tells Hansel to wait behind a tree and walks up the path and knocks on the door. The witch lets her in. Hansel is frightened. The house of candy has swallowed her up. After a while the door reopens. Gretel calls out, 'It' all right, little Hansel. You can come in now.' But the witch frightens him. He runs back home to his wicked stepmother. When he grows to be a man, he will fight them all. But Gretel doesn't run, she stays on.
>
> (*FF* 93)

The story sounds familiar. Of course it is the story of Hansel and Gretel, but it reads different. Isn't it Hansel who should be the stronger of the two, and Gretel who should get frightened and run away? Well, what's happening here and where did the narrator go wrong? On closer analysis we find that the narrator here has not gone wrong but is righting the wrong in addressing the gender bias of the original story. That is what Suniti Namjoshi's tales often do: Invoke the familiar world of fairly tales and fables, empty them of their original patriarchal content and charge them with new meanings underscoring the need for reviewing old worlds and stereotypical modes of perception and representation. To examine the existing systems of thought, to interrogate the texts and contexts of male authority, and to offer alternate modes of cognition and perception – these are among the prime concerns of Namjoshi's creative work. She achieves these by changing the place and place value of things, by re-telling old tales from shockingly new perspectives, by subverting all forms of authority, and by unsettling all conventional notions of order.

Namjoshi's re-visionist writing may best be viewed as a part of contemporary women writers' rejection of traditional narratives. Rachel Blau DuPlessis, in *Writing Beyond the Ending*, sees this revisionary critique as a major thread in the work of twentieth century women writers:

> There is a consistent project that unites some twentieth – century women writers across the century, writers who examine how social practices surrounding gender have entered narrative, and who consequently use narrative to make critical statements about the psychosexual and socio-cultural construction of women.... Writing beyond the ending means the trangressive invention of narrative strategies, strategies that express critical dissent from dominant narrative.
>
> (1985: 4-5)

Transgression is the key to transformation here, and appropriation turns into expropriation. Much of Namjoshi's work is marked by artful transgressions of standard narrative in thematic, technical and narratorial terms. Such transgressions necessitate an ironic vision, an ability to imagine beyond the limits of the so called "normal" and "standard", and an intent for transformational change. The best part of this transformative exercise of Namjoshi lies in the general mood of playfulness in which it is all done.

This strong impulse to look at life from a different angle, to interrogate conventional value systems, and to make fresh and original discoveries seems to have guided not only her creative work, but also all her major decisions in life. She has lived life differently right from the beginning. Namjoshi, born in a highly influential Chitpavan Brahmin family of Pune, was determined to be somebody in her own right and she was hardly twenty-three when she qualified for the Indian Administrative Service, the most highly regarded government position even today. But even as a young adult she was not enamoured of the plum job and the power it brought. As she herself put it, she was "bored" once "she figured out how to stay out of trouble." She then took study leave to pursue a master's program in Public Administration at the University of Missouri, Columbia. In 1969 she resigned from the Administrative service and moved to Montreal, Canada to do a Ph. D. at McGill. She worked on modern poetry and was awarded doctoral degree for her thesis: 'Ezra Pound and Reality: The Metaphysics of the Cantos.' Namjoshi's serious preoccupation with the question of reality seems to have begun at this stage. Besides, the modernist penchant for experimental constructs too has inspired her own creative work considerably. Namjoshi taught courses in literature at Scarborough College, Toronto University for the next fifteen years.

A major shift in her career as well as creative life occurred during the first sabbatical she spent in London and Cambridge between 1978-79 when she came under the influence of Feminist and Gay Liberation movements which provided her the idiom to define and articulate her own beliefs and inner compulsions. This was a period of intense introspection for Namjoshi. She defined and developed for herself strong political and ideological positions that manifest in and sustain her later poetic and fictional compositions. In 1988, she resigned her teaching position and moved to Devon where she presently lives and writes. A refusal to be bound by conventional roles, a restless striving after reality, a quest for alternate modes of perception and expression mark her life and work.

Namjoshi's literary career began with the publication of a slim volume of poems in 1967. These are poems on random themes, but reveal the unusual sensitivity of the author. In the same year she also published *Poems of Govindagraj* which she translated from Marathi with her mother Sarojini Namjoshi. Another two anthologies of poems of Namjoshi, *More Poems* and *Cyclone in Pakistan* came out in 1971, and these early attempts are characteristic of some of the vital traits of her more mature work. Namjoshi blends incisive insights into personal emotions and feeling with almost clinical analyses of socio-cultural institutions and systems.

It is with the publication of *The Jackass and the Lady* that Namjoshi consolidated her poetic achievement. By this time Namjoshi's political development is complete and she comes out openly and boldly with clear indications of her own ideological positions as a feminist and a lesbian. Her inner impulses and sexual preferences camouflaged in symbolic cocoons so far are now laid open, and some of her most powerful and evocative verses are found in this collection. Namjoshi's next collection of poems *The Authentic Lie* published two years later focuses on the theme of death and is rich in metaphysical speculations. This poem is autobiographical and deals with her own childhood grief on losing her father. As signified by the title *The Authentic Lie*, this collection is rich in paradoxical thought and expression, and reflects the philosophical disposition of the poet's mind.

It is after more than a decade's poetic work that Namjoshi turns to fiction writing. Generic differences are not of any paramount importance to her. She deliberately transgresses generic conventions to drive home the point that literary conventions are also constructs and constructs that often conceal dominant ideologies of class and gender. Namjoshi has always had a fascination for fables and fairy-tales and indulged in de-constructive readings of these texts playfully exposing the discriminatory practices that informed these apparently harmless children's stories. In *From the Bedside Book of Nightmares* she rewrites Shakespeare's *The Tempest*, the canonical text of colonial interactions, from the perspective of female Caliban thus launching a two-fold attack on racial and gender exploitation.

Namjoshi has always preferred symbolic and allegorical mode to realistic presentation. She increasingly makes fantasy and fabulation her base to launch a satiric attack on the anomalies she finds in the world around her. The use of fantasy in subversive fiction, particularly in feminist subversion of gender constructs, has been critically noted. To quote Nancy Walker, it is "the combination of fantasy and irony – particularly fantasy viewed ironically – that constitutes a fundamental critique of cultural realities in the contemporary novel by women" (1990: 7). Feminist writers like Ursula Le Guin, Angela Carter, Jody Scott, Margaret Atwood have all moved away from realism since they believe that the reality that the so-called realist literature represents is the patriarchal reality flawed by gender bias. They use fantasy to explore areas of life that realist literature tends to deny or repress, and forge concepts and ideas that contradict patriarchal ideology. Namjoshi uses fantasy as a technique of defamiliarization in *The Conversations of Cow* (1985) and *The Mothers of Mayadiip* (1989).

Her strength as a fabulist lies in crafting fantastic and farcical situations. She creates strange 'Looking Glass Countries' where things happen in an apparently bizarre fashion, but reveal interesting patterns on a closer analysis. All fiction is in some sense fantasy in that it is an imaginative construction, but the pervasive use of fantasy as an organizing principle and mode of perception as in the case of Namjoshi's work suggests an overwhelming need for imaginative release from objective reality. To quote Rosemary Jackson: "The fantastic traces the unsaid and the unseen of culture: that which has been silenced, made invisible, covered over and made absent" (1981: 3-4).

Fantasy also provides Namjoshi suitable fictional space for unfolding narratives of lesbian desire and experience. Namjoshi is the first Indian woman writer to have openly declared her sexual choice as a lesbian and has since held that the kind of sexual life one chooses to lead is a purely personal matter, where an individual's autonomy should neither be checked nor curtailed. She views compulsory heterosexuality as a repressive social structure that systematically subordinates women and reduces them to the status of 'the other' in a male dominated socio-cultural system.

Namjoshi has always stayed off the limelight and shunned publicity. She is not one of the frequently interviewed writers, nor has she published any personal statements. The only book where Namjoshi directly discusses her own personal experiences and contexts in which her texts took shape is *Because of India* (1989). Here Namjoshi has put together selections from all her creative work -- verse and fiction, -- written in the two decades following her first publication in 1967, and retrospectively explored the connections between her life and her work. *Because of India* is structured chronologically and divided into ten sections. Each section includes poems/prose fables/extracts from a single text and the author's reflections on the selections as well as situations in which these were written. The title of this important anthology hints at Namjoshi's strong bond with India and this volume may be viewed as the expatriate writer's grateful tribute to her mother country. The biographical information made available in this book is suitably used in my discussions of individual texts in later chapters.

The most important contribution of Namjoshi to

contemporary Indian fiction in English lies in creating an active, responsible and participating reader. No reader of Namjoshi's work is ever allowed to remain passive and complacent; the writer indulges in parodic and metafictional writing and weaves a whole lot of intertextual allusions into her work. In doing so she lays bare the accepted literary conventions and codes. The reader, therefore, must accept responsibility for the act of decoding. Her novels do not provide an order and meaning that readers can readily recognize. Instead they demand that the reader be conscious of the work, the actual construction that he/she too is undertaking because it is the reader who concretizes the work and gives it life. Namjoshi's most recent novel *Building Babel* directly co-opts readers into co-authorship in the process of building Babel.

Another important issue Namjoshi addresses explicitly in *Building Babel* and implicitly in a good deal of her earlier work is the power of language to both control and subvert authority. The issue of women's language is the subject of much contemporary debate and the need for women writers to reclaim a language of their own free from the influence of male conceptualizing is often stressed. For some critics such as Helene Cixous language is tied intimately to gender, "Woman must write woman. And man, man" (1976: 877). Female writing is bound up in female biology, she maintains, because women have been taught to feel guilty about both, and the courage to claim and proclaim both language and biology is for her the first step toward "transformation". Sisters engaged in Babel building in Namjoshi's *Building Babel* too are inspired by a similar vision. They analyse the situation thus:

> "The problem is we've all been typecast"
> "The problem is God"
> "No, no, the problem is man!"
> "The problem is us. For original sin/Look within."
> "The problem is mother!"
> "The problem is words!"
>
> (*BB* 29)

A quest for new words, therefore, becomes an important aspect of women's movement for liberation.

Another important motif in Namjoshi's work is identity or selfhood -- concepts that are particularly complex in an era in which feminist psychology poses challenges to Freudian and post-Freudian theories of human development. Women writers contest the notions of self that are forged by traditional psychoanalysis and quest for alternative selves. Self-definition therefore becomes an important concern for them. Namjoshi shares the feminist concern for identity politics; but rejects the notion of a unitary self. Instead she endorses the concept of plural and shifting selves. Such a notion is in consonance with the Hindu concept of transmigration of souls and it enables her to de-construct not only gender-hierarchy but also hierarchization of living species.

Namjoshi's work -- poetical as well as fictional -- despite its overtly political designs is more than a literature of protest. It is provocative, engaging and entertaining. Fantasies, excursions into strange places, free traffic between animal and human worlds, outrageous inversions of all accepted notions of order are delightfully inventive. Wit both defensive and offensive is acid, and flamboyant comedy efficiently exposes the anomalies in contemporary social structures. Since Namjoshi's work insists on the relativity and mutability of truth and reality and defies fixity of meaning, it is ingenuous to attempt any definitive readings or interpretations of her texts. This study, therefore, will try to contextualize Namjoshi's work within the broad spectrum of women's writing and other oppositional discourses and examine her contribution to the creation of alternate worlds, verbal, textual and conceptual, which once imagined become possible potential places to dwell in future.

Works Cited

Cixous, Helene. "The Laugh of the Medusa." Trans. Keith Cohen and Paula Cohen. *Signs*. 1.4 (Summer 1976): 875-93.

DuPlessis, Rachel Blau. *Writing Beyond the Ending: Narrative Strategies of Twentieth-Century Women Writers*. Bloomington: Indiana University Press, 1985.

Jackson, Rosemary. *Fantasy: The Literature of Subversion*. London: Methuen, 1981.

Namjoshi, Suniti. *Feminist Fables*. London: Sheba Feminist Publishers, 1981.

—. *Building Babel*. Melbourne: Spinifex, 1996.

Walker, Nancy A. *Feminist Alternatives*. Jackson and London: University of Mississippi Press, 1990.

2

Early Poems

Some of the poetic qualities which are to emerge more strongly in Namjoshi's later work are discernible in her early poems included in the first three published volumes of her poetry *Poems* (1967), *Cyclone in Pakistan* (1971) and *More Poems* (1971). For instance, her predilection for introspection and self-analysis and her strong concern with the social networks around her have run parallel in her poetic work right from the beginning. Besides, her incisive analysis of the various systems that control human lives and relationships, her penchant for re-reading myths from newer perspectives, her preoccupation with sexuality and her preference for paradoxical statements and willful obfuscation may also be traced to some of the verses included in these early anthologies. Namjoshi's movement towards a liberal praxis, intellectualism and philosophic speculation begins in these early poems.

Her first collection, *Poems*, is a curious anthology that has no unifying theme but contains the poet's musings on a number of related and unrelated issues ranging from the memory of a dead friend to a policeman and an aphrodisiac. Performance of the poet in this maiden attempt is uneven, yet promising. Namjoshi comes up with brilliant verse highly suggestive and evocative, but lapses into dull and dense poetry at times. However, all the poems, whether they work or not, reflect an intellect that refuses to be content with a mundane living and is intent on exploring the enigma of life. A restless and persistent mind that questions, probes and quests informs these verses. One notices a strangely felt tension between the logical workings of the reason and and non-logical associations of the intuition in these early attempts of a young poet probing the paradoxes of life. The doubt, tentativeness and ambivalence that mark most poems in these anthologies anticipate the open-ended nature of the vision of Namjoshi that is to emerge more completely in her later work.

Namjoshi's first collection, *Poems*, contains twenty four poems, and most of these poems are intensely personal and express a young woman's deep dissatisfaction with the given world and order of things, and her strong awareness of the need for a transformational change. Titles of some of the poems in this collection -- 'The Lesson', 'Apology', 'Various Reasons', 'Disturbance', 'Flawed' -- indicate the poet's propensity for intellection and rational analysis. Namjoshi frames an almost cynical sequitur in these poems. She raises questions but refrains from offering any definitive answers. In fact, she already seems to feel that there are no neat and final answers to the dilemmas of life. Consider these lines:

> Was it courage or fear that kept us silent
> Watching the dragonfly over the water?
>
> ("The Head of the Rose" *P* 5)

Or her prayer to God:

> Merciful God, you taught us the meaning of guilt
> And the world taught us how to trouble ourselves
> With the pursuit of happiness.

Truly, oh God, betwixt you both,
We have learnt how to suffer.

("The Lesson" *P* 5)

At each stage her statements and counter-statements make for a double helix, nodes and anti-nodes in interference-wave structures. Fortunately the poet does not get entangled in a double-bind; instead enjoys a liberation through articulation of the enigmas in a series of conundrums. Once that is done she lets the utterances tussle with each other and leaves the responsibility of resolution to the reader. Monica Varma, one of the earliest commentators on Namjoshi's work, aptly describes this aspect of her poetry when she says: "...she lets the whole image, concept, idea run like sand through her fingers – and then you know she has dusted her fingers and walked away, but walked away to life and not to a going away" (1973: 4).

The most distinctive quality of Namjoshi's early verse is the great economy of words. In short four line poems she often manages to pack intense personal reflections and even philosophical insights. 'On Stage' exemplifies this complete restraint the poet effectively exercises.

In a wine glass I float,
Whoever I be,
And the person who sits talking to them
Is the person They see.

(*P* 9)

Her preference for suggestive and symbolic forms of expression is obviously necessitated by the contrapuntal movement in her verse. In carefully crafted images she articulates her own inner perplexities and conflicts and conveys her perceptions of life and experience. Her penchant for symbolic mode is best exemplified in 'Red Flower'. It begins on a note of critical objectivity as the persona approaches the red flower with a scientific finger. As she strips the petals one by one, there is a transfer of meaning by which stripping the flower becomes a sexual act of stripping human body.

> There's a kind of beauty
> In the corpse of love, freshly picked
> And the juice still held in the petals.

The poet then comments on contemporary social/sexual norms and stresses that "the complex mind/Sees infidelity only as a symptom/Of passion" (*P* 8).

Namjoshi's symbolism sometimes becomes too personal to be accessible to a reader, and this results in the characteristic ambiguity of her verse. For instance 'Terra and the Speculator' runs thus:

> Being chivalrous, he ignored the stains on her dress,
> Told her politely, "You're a lovely planet.
> All your children are such good-looking youngsters,
> Sure to do well." But she didn't answer
> And the observer fell asleep on her breast.
>
> (*P* 8)

Commenting on these lines, Monica Varma, rightly remarks: "It is a little mad – but surely poets must be allowed an extra allowance of lunacy – but it is delicious all the same" (1973: 4).

Some of Namjoshi's poems are extraordinarily gentle and articulate tender feelings of love and contentment. The persona in "When I Die I Might be Rich", for instance, expresses her indebtedness to rich treasures of nature in moving terms. She begins by surmising on her own death:

> When I die I might be rich.
> A lawyer might come to my stately home
> And make an inventory, a collection of records,
> A collection of books, valuable perhaps?
> Odds and ends, paintings, tables and chairs.
>
> (*P* 16)

At this point a sudden shift of perspective occurs. While the countable material riches are accountable, invaluable natural wealth she had enjoyed all her life is beyond all reckoning. She gratefully acknowledges her debt to nature thus:

> But the things on which I had a lease-hold,
> Trees, grass, and blue-sky;
> And those I consumed free,
> Clear water and sun, friendship and love,
> Who's to account for them?

The last line, paradoxical in import, captures a moment of apprehension of the greater paradox, that is, life.

> Midway
> Through my wealth, I acknowledge my debt.
>
> (*P* 16)

Although Namjoshi does not talk much about the influence of Hindu philosophy on her, some of her most casual sounding remarks are deeply informed by her Hindu heritage. In an early poem called "Epitaph", for instance, she addresses a dead friend and wonders how she should comprehend the fact of death. She answers her own dilemma drawing on the Hindu belief in the eternity of soul:

> My friend you live in twisted mazes,
> In the back-slapping of the I and Not-I,
> In old wounds and little shames,
> Integral part of memory and mind.
>
> (*P* 6)

Again "Once I Saw" a seemingly simple personal poem narrating the recollection of the poet's childhood visit to the Ganga, echoes Hindu faith in the ultimate oneness of all forms of existence, the cardinal principle of the *advaita*. The poem begins by positing the difference between "us" (the poet and her two brothers) and "those others" who "come to Kashi to be cleansed". As children they are unaware of the truth that "the throng in the temple was us," and they never guessed that "the corpse/In the river was us". However, when the boatman ferries them over to the place where weavers lived and worked, they realise that all lives are after all interwoven as warp and woof on the loom of life ("Once I saw", *P* 10). Once you see lattices and patterning, you realise that patterning can be infinite weaving and bonding that may not be limited except by the number of elements of the set or by adoption of limitations.

"In English" is a sensitive analysis of the cultural dilemmas experienced by an Indian poet writing in English. The images which come naturally to an Indian poet whether it is ambergris, attar or silk, bullock cart, cock or pan are most likely to evoke a sense of exocita in foreign readers. How does an Indian write in English without arousing an orientalist response? The poet exclaims in exasperation:

> Oriental princess,
> How can I make these foreigners understand you are my mother?
> (*P* 10)

One of Namjoshi's favourite poetic themes has been death, and she probes the inevitability of this final termination with a rare courage. For instance, "The Death of Old Adam" begins thus:

> An old man died in a field of tulips,
> The nervous energy gone.

The poet then goes on to examine how one strives and struggles despite knowing death is an unavoidable fact of life. Analysing this paradox, Namjoshi says:

> Now dirt is dead and hurt is dead.
> Not getting is dead.
> There's nothing to get.
> (*P* 9)

Death, therefore, can be viewed as a release from the human

struggle to live. To speculate on the theme of death, Namjoshi aptly makes Adam her symbol. Adam is not only the first man, but also is responsible for bringing death into the world. Was that a curse or a boon?

The essential Namjoshi, however, is neither serious nor otherworldly. She is at her best when she indulges in a seemingly irreverant play with the traditional, the conventional and the sacred. Namjoshi's playful preoccupation with the old tales and her de-constructive readings of these texts may be seen in poems such as "Beauty and the Beast", "The Unicorn" and "Cain". To Namjoshi, Cain and Abel do not symbolize the binaries of evil and good as the mythical text suggests, but are "Two souls lodged in one body." Any rigid separation of these two souls and two worlds is sophistry. Namjoshi prefers schizophrenic battle within the divided self to such sophistry. The mythical unicorn traditionally considered a symbol of chastity and fierceness, and supposedly tamed by the touch of a virgin is a favorite symbol with Namjoshi, since it gives her a handle to demolish the patriarchal notions of female chastity.

* * *

In her next volume, *More Poems*, Namjoshi begins to bring animals into her poetic domain. This tendency to people her world with animal characters grows stronger with each work, and in some of her later work blue donkeys and one-eyed monkeys occupy the centre stage. Another significant feature of this collection is Namjoshi's increasing preoccupation with the mythical and fabular worlds depicted in the stories of the past. Besides, a number of these poems reflect her immediate concerns as an Indian woman living in Canada. Although Namjoshi published major portion of her creative work after she had moved out of India, she rarely confronts the fact of her immigrant living in her poetry. *More Poems* is one collection where themes of dislocation and diasporic living dominate, and the expatriate poet's fears of living in an alien land amidst strangers are voiced. Motifs of journey, expatriation and experience of alienation recur in this volume. Namjoshi appropriately describes the loss of self-identity one experiences as a foreigner in an alien land thus:

> First,
> You take off your clothes,
> Your titles and name
> And put on a robe
> Sterile and clean,
> With neat black letters
> Marking THE STRANGER.
>
> Then,
> You walk down the street,
> Alone in fancy dress
> ("How to be a Foreigner", *MP* 14)

An occasional tone of nostalgia is struck in poems like "The Old Country Says" and "My Aging Country". In the former the poet considers the predicament of a nation which loses its youth to "strange new lands". The poem begins with the old country saying,

> My young people are all out,
> Voyaging through strange lands.

But in the end the country sounds content:

> And now they are all out
> And have grown well.
>
> (*MP* 12)

This reveals the typical expatriate ambivalence: Is moving out a loss or gain? Migration, after all, is a complex experience of loss and gain: for a tradition lost, there is the newly won freedom to live life on ones own terms; for the security of home and family sacrificed, there are possibilities of assimilation and acquisition; for an anchorage severed, there is the delight of discovery. The author who has moved out and done well seems to transfer her own personal feelings of contentment to the nation. A similar mood of ambivalence marks the poem: "My Aging Country". The persona here is obviously an expatriate Indian whose reverence for her ancient country is hued by a touch of regret at its present state. The confusion of the speaker is revealed in the very opening lines of the poem:

> How shall I take you,
> Having no handle?

The play on the word handle is significant. As an expatriate who is cut off from her aging country, she knows she wields no power. However, her love for home is unmistakable.

> You are beautiful,
> In a blue sea.
> ....
> And I love you.
>
> (*MP* 18)

Somewhere in the depths her mind the speaker has misgivings about the present state of her country. She, therefore, asks:

> You really don't think
> You might smarten yourself?
>
> (*MP* 18)

But the speaker is afraid of hurting the sentiments of her ancient land and is willing to love the aging country as it is. A strong sense of love and longing for the home country left behind, and a disconcerting realization that immigration after all had not been a bad bargain create a sort of conflict which often shades into a feeling of guilt.

Distance, separation, loss and longing are more poignantly expressed in "The Elsewhere Fish". The persona here is unable to bridge the gap between the country she left behind and the one she lives in. As Jasbir Jain, rightly observes: "the two countries become the two countries of the mind, of belonging or not belonging, of being left out and being involved" (1991: 116). "Letter" is another short poem that deals with the need to communicate across temporal and spatial distance, across "miles of ocean and days in time". The poem ends with the plea:

> And I open my mind thus and thus
> And say, 'if it should please you,
> Come and spend little time with me.'
>
> (*MP* 25)

The past that the poet has left behind surfaces and reasserts itself in her poems. In "Past Matters" Namjoshi compares the poet to a frogman "who swims below to look at the old sea-dead," a priest who "considers wherein lay betrayal," and a jig-saw puzzler who "idles with pieces of his mind" (*MP* 20). Diving into one's past, probing one's own guilt and assembling the fragments of one's mind are a part of poetic creation. Sometimes every thing including writing poetry appears meaningless to Namjoshi as she is perplexed by the contradictions that mark human existence. "Sick in a Strange Country" registers one such moment of emotional fatigue and despair:

> Life is an exercise in living
> I'm sick and needn't say
> Anything that makes sense at all.
>
> (*MP* 34)

This withdrawal is temporary; her engagement with life is so intense that the enigma of existence continues to evoke in her poetic responses. "Rationale" exemplifies Namjoshi's predilection for serious philosophic speculation. Here she visualizes the entire business of living as treading the delicate balance between life and death:

> How exquisitely we're balanced between life and death,

Willing to live, not unwilling to die,

(*MP* 31)

One therefore need fear neither life nor death.

There are poems in this anthology which reveal Namjoshi's perceptions of the West, especially America. A tone of unmistakable irony runs through her short poem "Columbia, America". The perfect orderliness of the city makes no allowance for any deviations. Everything is expected to be in place: houses, trees and squirrels all seem to fit in properly. However,

..... the only jarring note
Is a bird in bad taste
Lying dead on the street.

The speaker ironically concludes: "Accidents will happen" (*MP* 15). 'The New York Bird' is even more critical of the materialism of America. The poet sarcastically comments on America's capacity to commodify everything and obtain monopoly over its manufacture. The speaker here wryly states:

In accordance with my duty
I caught the New York Bird and opened
His heart to learn what made him tick.
Now we have a factory for New York Birds.
Though two inch beaks are no longer worn.

(*MP* 17)

Sometimes Namjoshi touches upon the politics of colonization and racism albeit in a passing manner. For instance, 'Those Astonishing Anglo-Saxons' is a brief and direct statement on the Anglo-Saxon occupation of Americas:

Somebody said:
Here is a country
With all the amenities
Land of free air, water to drink,
One wild beast,

> The horrid grizzly bear,
> Two dread snakes, the python and the rattle
> Indians and squaws,
> Quakes and tornadoes
> Go forth and live.
> They did.
>
> (*MP* 13)

The facts of history thus baldly stated expose the distortions of colonial rhetoric and lay bare the absurdity of the whole project of colonial expansion. "A Problem" is a poem about racism and it powerfully brings out the subtle ways in which racial discrimination operates. The poem begins with the question: "Can a body hurt a body?" and this direct question is answered indirectly, yet unambiguously as the speaker goes on to explain:

> Place a foreign body
> In a given element.
> Put on new glasses
> To blot out your sight
> When you find a given body
> In a foreign element.
> Oh, look, it would seem
> Assimilative America
> Has a mote in her eye
>
> (*MP* 36)

A strong suspicion of the political designs of neo-colonial power centres is directly stated in these lines. The questions of power and domination are of special concern to all postcolonial writers and politics is very much a part of their poetic preoccupations. Namjoshi's poetry, which is generally suggestive, complex and symbolic, sheds its artifice completely while raising political issues.

Namjoshi's poems are rich in intertextual cadences and often read and misread literary texts of the past. Some of her poems, in the Bloomean sense, are "neither about 'subject' nor about themselves but about other poems" (1975: 18). But when she re-reads an earlier literary work she does so not to belong to that larger literary tradition, but to bring it under interrogation. For instance "Theatre of the Absurd in Toronto" is rich in intertextual mis/readings. The sub-life of the sub-way is "Like the sub-life of the stage" and this at once brings to our mind Shakespeare's description: "All the world is a stage." While Shakespeare noted there are entrances and exits in the play of life, the sub-play of Namjoshi is "without an end or start". The great bard talked about each playing a part in the play of life, and Namjoshi adds to this philosophic comment a curiously commercial twist when she says:

> Where each of us *sans pay*
> Performs a little part,
>
> (italics mine, *MP* 28)

Playing with old texts and rewriting them in parodic tones is one of Namjoshi's favourite techniques.

"It's a Quality of the Gods" invokes the famous mercy speech of Portia in Shakespeare's *The Merchant of Venice*. While Shakespeare describes 'mercy' as a Divine quality, Namjoshi subverts the whole argument when she says:

> It's a quality of the gods
> To see a creature with its back broken
> And be unmoved.
> ....
> The gods are unafraid
> And the gods are unbroken,
> And cannot love and cannot grieve.
>
> (*MP* 32)

Here is a curious case of re-visionism where in an Indian woman poet enters a Western male canonical text from a new critical direction. A more detailed analysis of Namjoshi's re-visionist re-reading is attempted in subsequent chapters.

Some of the best poems in this collection are those charged with strong sexual suggestions. Namjoshi often celebrates desire and sexual fulfilment in her intensely evocative verse. "Pinocchio", for instance, takes the long nosed hero of the nursery tales for its central character. The persona recalls the image of Pinocchio from her childhood memory, but it comes back to her charged with new meanings and newer possibilities. As she encounters Pinocchio anew in her adulthood, she is in fact apprehensive that she might "smudge the miracle" with her fingertips. In fact it is much safer to conceal desire under a powdered mask than confront it. It is harmless if Pinocchio remains "a ghost", "a dream" or "a doll". But this illusion of innocence is sure to be shattered sometime, and it would then be imperative for her and Pinocchio "to move/To the other side of curtain" (*MP* 10). Namjoshi here focuses on the reality of desire and the illusion of innocence.

* * *

Cyclone in Pakistan another slim volume of poems which also appeared in the same year, 1971, reveals Namjoshi's preoccupation with social issues such as poverty, deprivation, war, violence and loss of life. Recalling the background to writing of these verses Namjoshi says: "I was acquiring the beginnings of a social conscience, or perhaps it was only a social consciousness. The real teaching experience had to do with feeling in my lived life what it was like to be poor to the point of wondering what one was going to eat. There was also the matter of experiencing the social hierarchy at the bottom end of the system." (1989: 21). A large number of poems in *Cyclone in Pakistan* sound angry, and voice Namjoshi's serious indictment of the goings on in the world around her. The title poem, for instance, is about the 1970 cyclone in Pakistan. The poem reports the death of 100,000 human beings in the cyclone, and describes how corpses were thrown up by the sea. Then it records a cold materialistic response to this human tragedy:

Sea-sodden corpses
are useful to no one.
200,000 eyeballs
never to be grafted.

A quick scientific suggestion then pops up:

Next time it happens
We'll have a freezer ready.

("Nov. 1970 Cyclone in Pak" *CP* 12)

The speaker here deliberately shocks the reader through use of gruesome images. This is specifically intended to break the apathy and insensitivity pervading human interactions. Shockingly ghastly images in Namjoshi's poetry are a deliberate strategy to shatter the complacency under which people generally try to take shelter.

"Sanitation" too is written in the same tone. The poem begins with the question:

What shall we do with the poor,
The diseased and the sentimental?

These are grouped with different forms of wastage such as "cellophane and wrappers", "the cars and scrap" "exhaust from our lungs" etc. The reply comes in decisive terms:

Let's make a clean sweep,
Powder the trees,
Grind the boxes, animal boxes
Reduce the mountain to rubble.

(*CP* 10)

The sweep of cleaning of course implies we get rid of the poor, the diseased and the sentimental as well. Namjoshi's satire acquires sharper tone in some of her short poems like "Hiatus". The entire poem is quoted here:

The well-dressed man, who flogged the hag,
who killed the child, suddenly stopped, and asked,

"Doesn't the number of dead ever bother you?"
(*CP* 12)

There are poems in this anthology which articulate Namjoshi's responses to literature. "In Defense" is a poetic tribute to Swift's sensitivity to the crimes of the contemporary society. There is a poem for Ezra Pound who was the subject of Namjoshi's doctoral work. She confesses to Pound that although she has almost become one with him in many ways, there are realities that belong to her part of the world which continue to engage her:

So, I read you
And write
Something else
("For E.P." *CP* 20)

Having gone through the various movements in literary thought, as a student of literature, she sometimes makes critically ironic observations on these theoretical developments. Literary theory had announced the death of God and the death of the author. What is left after that? Namjoshi remarks:

Listen fellows, big poets, small poets,
what you ought to be doing
is practising hard
for the death of the world.
("For the Occasion" *CP* 11)

Namjoshi often indulges in poetic speculations on the very process of poetic creation. This predilection for metatextual musings places her in the category of contemporary postmodernist writers. For instance, 'Whittler' is about the very act of creation. The poet is a whittler since he/she is engaged in whittling, chiseling and shaping in order to create a work of art, call it a "doll" "talisman" "poem" or "wares". All art is, after all, a moment recaptured.

The doll is a moment,
recapturing a moment.
The doll is a poem.

(*CP* 18)

In a typical Namjoshi move, she then breaks the tempo she builds with a sudden shift of perspective.

Ah no, the doll is my wares,
You pay with a smile.

(*CP* 18)

There are a number of short 2-4 line poems in these early collections which express the poet's quick and spontaneous responses to the world around her. Monica Varma calls them "literary doodles" and describes them as instances of "Tukbands" "a short statement in verse" "with no pretensions of being kavya or poetry. She attributes Namjoshi's failure to be "poetic" to some dissonance in the poet's personal experience which creates a corresponding dissonance in her poetic expression. Varma is obviously judging Namjoshi's poetry according to certain preconceived notions about the nature of poetry, but it is important to note that Namjoshi is out to demolish all such preconceptions and hence the so called dissonance. Varma is however, justified in pointing out that some of Namjoshi's short poems end up as bold statements of no avail. This happens in poems such as "QED" and "Old Fame". I quote "Contemporary" in full as an instance of a prose poem turning into mere prose:

The government official
speaks in English with friend,
in Hindi with servants,
and reserves his mother tongue
for his 2 Alsatian dogs.

(*CP* 14)

But "Altitudes" and "Small Point", short as they are, set the reader thinking by stating a little and leaving a lot to readers' speculations. The reader in Namjoshi's work is never expected to be a passive recipient of ideas, sermons and messages. Her way of communication has always been through hints, clues and suggestions and much is left to the imagination of the reader. Sometimes this brevity results in ambiguity, and some of her two line poems end up as quizzical statements of no significance. Consider these lines:

> Does the old, fierce sun that blazed for us
> Now burn alone for your sole pleasure?
>
> (*CP* 14)

This puzzle-like poem does not even enthuse the reader to make an effort to probe or speculate on the possibilities of meaning implied. Namjoshi's penchant for word play too can be intrusive sometimes. For instance in poems like "Bureaucrat" and "Be Reasonable" she comes up with intelligent verse and play of word images resulting in vignettes and not vision.

While Namjoshi rarely speaks of personal emotions at this stage, when she does so she writes evocative verse which works very well. "Grace" is a good example of the kind. Here the truth condition and intellectuality merge, and the poem sensitively records a moment of epiphany, a moment of discovery of truth where all other feelings and emotions are subsumed and the human need for companionship and love is stressed. I quote this poem in full since it is one of the earliest instances of highly evocative verse that Namjoshi has written:

> To say, 'I love', and set my face and walk away
> Reconciles conscience,
> And to say, 'I have not failed you',
> Is a proud thing;
> But to say, I need you and am human
> 'Do not make me beg
> 'Nor ask for more than you would give,'
> Dissolves pride and other considerations
> In truth
>
> ("*Grace*" *MP* 26)

The aptly suggestive title "Grace" subtly erases the distinction between physical love and the Divine and spiritual love.

Namjoshi's poetry reflects a mind that is fragmented and at war with itself and the world around. However, the author has learnt to turn her confusion and dilemmas into a priceless asset on which her poetry draws. Poetry is, in fact, the means through which she tries to come to terms with her own dividedness and schizophrenic condition. She steps and slides between binaries and multiples without any undue anxiety to reconcile them. It is Namjoshi's insistent preoccupation with the conflictual aspects of life and living that mark out her work for serious critical consideration.

Works Cited

Bloom, Harold. *The Anxiety of Influence*. New York: Oxford University Press, 1973.

Jain, Jasbir. "Suniti Namjoshi: The Dual World of Her Early Poems." *Problems of Postcolonial Literatures and Other Essays*. Ed. Jasbir Jain. Jaipur: Printwell Publishers, 1991. 109-120.

Namjoshi, Suniti. *Poems*. Calcutta: Writers Workshop, 1967.

—. *More Poems*. Calcutta: Writers Workshop, 1971.

—. *Cyclone in Pakistan*. Calcutta: Writers Workshop, 1971.

—. *Because of India*. London: Only Women Press, 1989.

Varma, Monica. *Facing Four*. Calcutta: Writers Workshop, 1973.

3

The Conversion Poems: *The Jackass and the Lady* and *The Authentic Lie*

Namjoshi's poetry enters a new phase with the publication of her next two volumes of poetry: *The Jackass and the Lady* (1980) and *The Authentic Lie* (1982). These two collections clearly register a consolidation of her political and philosophical positions respectively. While *The Jackass* spells out Namjoshi's ideological positioning as a lesbian-feminist writer, *The Authentic Lie* demonstrates her vital links with the Hindu philosophical lineage. Eight years had intervened between the publication of earlier poems and the *Jackass* anthology and these were years of great change and transformation in Namjoshi's life. There are sharp transitions within the book from one verse to another. What happened, in fact, between the writing of these poems and their subsequent revision before publication too is crucial in her career. She came under the impact of the

Western feminist thought, more precisely the lesbian movement during this period.

The Jackass and the Lady was written between 1972-1976 and published in 1980. During this period Namjoshi was a full-time teacher at the University of Toronto and was working on her doctoral dissertation. By this time she had come to feel that writing poetry cannot be a desultory affair, a leisure-time activity, an occasional whimsical pursuit but needs to be cultivated as a vocation. She used to set aside four hours every day for her creative writing and the verses of *Jackass* thus came of her assiduous engagement with poetry. Namjoshi gives a detailed account of the background to the publication of this work in *Because of India*:

> An offer of publication by a small Canadian Press fell through and so the book wasn't published till 1980. By 1980 I was a feminist, and revised some of the poems accordingly. In some instances it was simply a matter of restoring the poems to their original form.
>
> (1989: 27)

Some of her innermost feelings and proclivities either as a feminist or a lesbian which often were camouflaged in symbolic outfits in her earlier work are now articulated in more direct and forceful verse.

Namjoshi by this time has had years of serious engagement with English literature. She had also lived in the West for a considerable length of time to have developed a sense of estrangement much talked about in diasporic writing. But in her case the initial alienation took a strange turn as she slowly began to realise that she was never going to blend completely into the culture of the West. A certain confluence of Western and Hindu influences, she knew was going to be a part of her experience and her poetic articulation. For Namjoshi the question of identity became crucial at this stage. As an Indian living and writing in a predominantly White world, as a woman working in a largely male academia, as a Hindu in an all-Christian world she was operating from a position of multiple liminalities. As she searched for a suitable subject position for herself she found the avatar of a beast the best to assume for her poetic explorations. Thus was created the Jackass, the poetic persona for Namjoshi soon to be joined by many other beasts: blue donkeys, cows, rabbits and so on.

Namjoshi explains her reasons for choosing birds and beasts to inhabit her poetic world at some length in her introduction to the section on *The Jackass and the Lady* in her later anthology *Because of India*. She seems to have arrived at this choice more through elimination and rejection of other forms and identities. She couldn't have been the prince, she didn't want to be the lady either. Namjoshi convincingly argues:

> ... in a humanist universe, which has been male-centered historically, women are 'the other', together with the birds and the beasts and the rest of creation. An identification with the rest of the creation, possibly with the whole of it, would only be logical; unless, of course, one wished to create a mirror image of the humanist universe, with woman at the centre, accepting the consequences of consigning everything else to 'the other'. But I don't want to be separated from the birds and the beasts, nor do I want to "humanise" them particularly.
>
> (1989: 28-29)

Choosing the beast-apparel, therefore, was not only a rejection of gender stereotyping but also an attempt to nullify hierarchization of living beings.

At this point one can clearly see the influence of Hindu philosophy on her thinking.

> To me a beast wasn't "bestial" in the Western sense. To me a bird or a beast was a creature like anyone else. Hinduism is after all pantheistic; and the popular notion of reincarnation attributes a soul to everyone. This may sound odd to Western ears, but for me, it was as familiar as it was unconscious. It was in the very air I had breathed while growing up.
>
> (1989: 28)

Beginning with *Jackass*, in all her subsequent work Namjoshi lets birds and beasts speak for her. Animals and human beings, love each other and live together unmindful of any class/gender divide. In fact she has a poem about the animals in her poetic forest in this collection. In "The Animals in this Forest" she declares: "The animals in this forest are incorrigibly friendly" and goes as to justify her preference for animal characters thus:

> "Why do beasts inhabit your mind?"
> They like it there.
>
> (*JL* 49)

Later in the same poem, Namjoshi unequivocally admits: "But bird, beast and fish is all that I am" and concludes with the summing up statement: "And bird, beast and fish is all my theme" (*JL* 49). It is of course clear that she is not merely stating her choice of poetic subject here, but celebrating the all pervasive principle of life.

The Jackass and the Lady is a crucial text in the evolution of Namjoshi's poetic oeuvre because it records clearly her political awakening as a lesbian-feminist writer and this positioning is to influence profoundly all the major thematic and formal choices of her later work. Some of her favourite themes – the burden of the past, the identity of individuals and the need for relationship where there is no other transcendence – begin to find their clarifying focus and centre here.

Verses in *The Jackass* are arranged in three sections: 'The Reluctant Cannibals', 'Homage to Circe' and 'The Overgrown Garden'. The poet invokes symbols, characters, ideas and ideologies of literary texts of the past and effects a deliberate rupture of the structures contained there in opening new spaces that can harbour alternative positions and identities. The epigraph to the first section runs thus:

> It is not, Father, I who have sinned.
> I beseech Thee take this whore from my side.
>
> (*JL* 10)

The Adamic complex to view Eve as evil stands exposed in Namjoshi's re-writing of this prayer for the first man. The Biblical mythology and imagery provide the backdrop to some of the verses in this section. *The Bible* as the high patriarchal text, and particularly 'Genesis' as a male-biased version of creation have come in for several revolutionary re-writings in the hands of feminist poets and critics. Namjoshi's 'Her Form in clear water' reworks the Biblical story of the fall of (wo)man thus:

> Her form in clear water made him
> raise his head.
> His length slid about her limbs. Eve
> in her turn
> encircled the snake, pressing her body
> to him.
> Curious coupling, brown snake and Eve,
> caught in a twist
> of the blind green coil being Adam
> and evil and Eve.
>
> (*JL* 13)

Namjoshi's Eve prefers to be coupled with the snake rather than remain chained to Adam and bear the badge of a fallen woman.

"Patriarchy perpetuates its deception through myths", complains Mary Daly in *Gyn/ecology* (1978: 44). Feminist writers have, therefore, probed patriarchal myths to dis-cover the hidden designs that are discriminatory against women. Some of the earliest instances of revisionist myth making of Namjoshi are found in the verses of *Jackass* anthology. Alice, Narcissus, Psyche, Circe and the Dragon appear in altered identities in these poems. For instance, Namjoshi's "Narcissus" is neither about "the dead sinner" nor about "the rejected lover" but about "the child who cried when a dog snatched its bone." (*JL* 15). Namjoshi rejects the classical myth of Narcissus as well as its psychoanalytical interpretation and is glad that

Narcissus has after all "blossomed in purple living flowers". She does not always invert an old story but invents and creates new myths in de-constructing tales that are phallic and phallocentric. In Namjoshi's version of the "Beauty and the Beast", Beauty loves the ugly beast in the hope that the latter would change into a prince some day. She "waited for his shape to change/And found there were two beasts in bed." (*JL* 29). The closure of a conventional tale thus altered, calls into question the norms upheld by the original.

There are three versions to Namjoshi's "Dragon story". In one version "she slays the dragon", and in another "he slays the dragon and they live ever after off the dragon's hide". In the third version

> .... they kill one another
> While the dragon applauds. This is not
> uncommon, but the audience doesn't know
> it has played its part.
>
> (*JL* 31)

In offering multiple versions of a conventional dragon story Namjoshi underscores the fluidity of textual structures as well as the constructs of reality they conjure up.

Namjoshi's "Pastoral" which retells the story of Polyphemus and Galatea from Ovid's *Metamorphoses* is another interesting instance of 'reading against the grain' or re-visioning of canonical texts. It is only natural that Ovid's work should engage Namjoshi's creative attention. In his own writing Ovid had held a critical dialogue with his literary past and invoked an unprecedented range of Greek and Latin texts restoring revisionary energy to the work of his ancestors. Namjoshi's shaggy Polyphemus makes a gift of golden graphes to Galatea but she is not attracted. He tries several ways to please her and finally finds her 'twin bear cubs' and she readily takes to these 'unlikely pets'. All attributes of good and bad, cruel and kind, wicked and friendly associated with various living beings are thus exposed as mere constructs. Bears make pets for maidens and Cyclops prove to be more civilized than human beings. In the third section of this poem the unrepentant Cyclops throws a challenge to the so called civilized world thus:

> Lady, since I have behaved badly you can
> whip me in public with my shirt off
> or my pants down. Undoubtedly I shall
> make a ludicrous figure. But were you aware?
> – Such barbarisms occur only in your homes.
>
> (*JL* 37)

Namjoshi not only redeems the weird figures of the ancient texts, but makes them rip away the masks that humans wear.

It is important to note that much of the pleasure these re-readings offer arises out of the writer's play with old texts – their plots, characters and morals. Namjoshi is fond of telling stories and she comes up with short and compelling tales in poems of four or five lines. She narrates the tale of the King of a Rainy Country thus:

> The king of a rainy country weeps round tears;
> thinks he's impotent, unable to make the sun
> shine. This is not a climate for kings, he says,
> Where are the azures, the greens and the purples?
> He says the people are unsmiling. It is
> an unroyal welcome.
>
> (*JL* 19)

Similarly Namjoshi's account of Gulliver's fascination for a giantess in the land of Brobdingnags makes delightful reading. Gulliver can only gaze up to her thighs until one day she picks him off the floor and takes him to her breast. He makes her body his home and habitation, and is willing to live as her personal worm. Fantasy runs wild: the giantess sets Gulliver to sail in a "tepid cup of tea" and he performs valiantly. The healthy giantess feeds him on a continuous supply of milk and wonders: "poor little nankeen,/will nothing make you grow?"

Then comes the optimistic closure: "I grow. I am growing. You should see me in her dreams" (*JL* 60). Fabulation and fabrication of fantastic tales are among the favourite preoccupations of Namjoshi.

There are a number of poems in this collection which deal with female sexuality and lesbian eroticism. In 'The Arbitrary Order,' for instance, the persona questions the rigidity of traditional sex roles and makes the point that sex oppression is basically the oppression of sex role-bearers, gendered beings. Namjoshi complains:

> The arbitrary order: ducks
> quenching in the pond.
> Drakes mounting them.
>
> (*JL* 34)

Even if some can perceive the possibility of a different order, they can not possibly talk about it in a world controlled by traditional norms of sexual behaviour. Although Namjoshi chooses to speak in symbolic riddles, her work is clearly in consonance with the ideas and ideologies of the radical feminist group of Kate Millet, Alison Jaegar, Rita Mae Brown and others. Like them she urges "a world of endless possibilities and protean selves" (Phelan 43).

Poems like "Metamorphoses", "An Explanation" "She Turns the Grass" contain overtly sexual images and communicate the poet's lesbian proclivities. "I Give Her the Rose" is among the earliest instances of Namjoshi's lesbian eroticism. The poem reads thus:

> I give her the rose with unfurled petals.
> She smiles
>   and crosses her legs.
> I give her the shell with the swollen lip.
> She laughs. I bite
>   and nuzzle her breasts.
> I tell her, "Feed me on flowers

with wide open mouths,"
and slowly,
she pulls down my head.

(*JL* 43)

To have written these lines about a woman's passion for another woman in the 80's when lesbian movement was meeting with resistance everywhere must have meant an act of courageous defiance -- defiance of all norms. It is interesting to recall what Caroline Halliday, a lesbian poet herself, said about lesbian eroticism in this context: "The lesbian erotic poem is not only about connections and explorations. It is also about celebration, about breaking taboos, naming what *is* and what *is ours*." Namjoshi's poems too celebrate the freedom of lesbian erotic feeling, and affirm lesbian relationships actual, physical and sexual. Using nature imagery to signify lesbian sexuality is in fact common and it suggests that lesbian sexuality is natural unlike the heterosexual behaviour which is culturally conditioned.

In "Homage to Circe", the poet pays a rich tribute to the arch sorceress – Circe. Circe's power over her lovers whom she turns into animals is complete, and is symbolic of the power of woman. Namjoshi gives a slight twist to the traditional tale in extolling the intimacy between Circe and her pets. Strong sexual understones echo in the lines that describe the relationship between Circe and her animal-turned-lovers. The snake fondly caresses her shoulders and the dog burrows its nose in her warm thighs. The persona here wishes to be admitted into the realm of Circe's love and therefore pleads:

I am all animals to you?
I could sit cat-like and gaze
sisterly.
I am all animals to you,
could offer myself
on a wide lily-pad.

This exhortation to Circe reaches its peak in the closing lines:

> Circe,
> all animals adore you,
> you are all things to each
> In the tutelary garden, at the continuous feast.
>
> (*JL* 45)

Circe thus symbolizes liberation from heterosexual norms and forges possibilities of alternative sexualities.

In this collection there are poems about poems: the poet talks of her own creative experience sometimes; she reacts to the apathy and indifference of critics and readers at times. 'From what does a poem grow' is a neat little verse which symbolically describes the genesis of a poem:

> It grows from my thumb,
> distends itself to spherical form
> and casts off gently toward the sun.
>
> (*JL* 56)

In "Lines Written in Dejection" Namjoshi voices her disillusionment with popular responses to poetry. She complains that people's interest is rarely aroused by poetic feats and flights:

> But this gorgeous gargantua, this poet's prodigy,
> This mammoth metaphor pleases nobody.
>
> (*JL* 57)

Yet the poet writes, as writing has a liberating impact on her. Namjoshi explains the compulsions that urge her to write as follows:

> And she wrote her poems because muteness
> terrified her,
> seeing, as she did, in the level lake water
> an upside down swan.
>
> ("And She Wrote Her Poems", *JL* 16)

Seeing is an important prerequisite to writing. Seeing the anomalies in the world around, one cannot remain mute but must articulate, and hence the poems.

There are occasional references to emigrant living and exilic experience in this anthology. The original identity lost, new unformed, the emigrees move about like "princes in exile". Her poem "Emigree" begins thus:

> "In my own country I was a princess" – "Yes, but this is not your own country, miss"

Not many options are open to these "princes in exile". These royal children must remain "mute, proud and undiscovered" (*JL* 18). Rarely, a note of loneliness is struck in poems like "When I Cry":

> When I cry my tears trickle into brine
> You never saw me cry.
> That was sea-water the wind carried off.
>
> (*JL* 22)

Namjoshi, however, turns her loneliness, isolation and marginalization into an advantage and gains for herself a double perspective straddling two different cultures.

Thus strategic shifting of perspectives and altering of stereotypical motifs becomes an important emancipatory strategy in Namjoshi's poetry. The shock of the imagery is due not merely to subversion of familiar figures of patriarchal myths but to the tone of confidence revealed here. This demands that the readers think anew and participate in the cognitive revolution urged by these verses. Quite often, Namjoshi disregards the literary conventions concerning the use of syntax, register and symbolic connotation. This enables her to violate the linguistic decorum which dictates in what contexts it is appropriate to use which words and which symbols represent what sort of reality. The result of these transgressions is a heightened ambiguity regarding the meaning of some of Namjoshi's verses. This may also be construed as privatization of meaning. Besides, violation of linguistic decorum is reflective of violation of all notions of patriarchal order.

* * *

The Authentic Lie (1982) is very different from *The Jackass* collection since the prime preoccupation of the poet here is not with life but with the reality of death. These may be described as personal poems as Namjoshi is reflecting on her own childhood experiences here. Her father who was a test pilot, was killed in a plane crash when she was hardly twelve. This childhood trauma remained with her and the agony of a bereaved child is turned into a poetic theme in *The Authentic Lie*.

In these poems Namjoshi attempts a mature analysis of her childhood grief and turns this into an occasion to speculate on various aspects of death including human perceptions of this mystery. The poem is divided into three sections: "Discourse with the Dead", "Assassins" and "The Authentic Lie". The first is a poignant account of a child's grief at the loss of a parent and the second section elaborates the theme of death at a more abstract level. The third is rich in philosophical undertones and highlights paradoxical nature of death.

Although Namjoshi is recounting her personal experience here, she chooses third-person narrative, and makes her verses rigorously impersonal. The personal is generalized. That is a mode of rationalization for coming to grips with one's self, and past experience, even terror. The terror of death is not the fact, but the implication: absence which induces and enables imagination, and constant brooding over a dead person leave one mentally enervated. Writing about this experience, therefore, has a thereaupatic influence and becomes a stress-coping strategy. The narrator is distanced from the grieving child by time, and therefore is able to look on the child's experience with a certain degree of objectivity. The narrative begins thus: "He died when she was ten in a distance country and therefore the dreams would not stop" (*AL* 12).

The bereaved child continues to make nightly journeys in her dreams in quest of her lost father. She is constantly haunted by the question:

> First a live man
> then a dead man:
> where is my father?
>
> (*AL* 13)

The agonized child misses her father in every detail of day-to-day life and longs for his return. She pleads with the lost father thus:

> While you were lost in the forest
> we lived in the world.
> Why don't you come back,
> walking
> toward us, by chance, as it were,
> covered with tendrils?
>
> (*AL* 14)

The bereaved daughter who is an adult now is aware that the return of the dead is a sinister affair. The childhood dream of the return of the dead father acquires a nightmarish quality somewhere along the line, and hence the daughter's confession: "I fear your presence" (15). The business of life stops for none; the memories of the dead are submerged in the hub of life. But somewhere in the depths of her heart lies hidden the possibility of seeking her father lost long ago.

In these speculations on death and the possibility of seeking the dead, Namjoshi's poetry acquires a rare lyricism, Tennysonian in its impact. The following excerpt illustrates this:

> That dream is a hook,

> it hauls us both
> To that dreamy no-place,
>
> where loss is no-loss,
> and your tiredness
> a failure.
>
> (*AL* 18)

In an analytical exploration of the fact of death, Namjoshi inevitably arrives at an insight gleaned from the Hindu thought and philosophy.

> Roll back the rock.
> Examine the cave.
> The body is gone,
> but the soul remains,
> trailing terror.
>
> (*AL* 23)

The eternity of human soul makes the fact of mortality of human body more tolerable and less painful. A close examination of the issues of mortality and immortablity, birth and death, existence and liberation etc. cannot be conducted without the consideration of another more important subject: God. In a rare moment of prayful reverence says Namjoshi:

> Slips from the hand of God
> the simple soul, without
> any clothes on, and without colour.
>
> (*AL* 25)

Such articulations of pure philosophical speculation are uncharacteristic of Namjoshi. Her method is to speak through images, symbols old and new, riddles and cryptic poetic suggestions. Her work, as Sherry Simon one of her early reviewers rightly describes, "contains several contradictions ...." "It is at once lucid and troubling, apparently transparent and yet opaque, forthright and emotionally murky" (1985: 267). But it is important to note that these 'contradictions' arise out of the poet's unwillingness to see fixed patterns in the complex, ever-changing flux that reality is.

Some of the poems in this anthology are charged with imagery of violence and hint at a rupture in personal relationships. For instance, the poet unleashes a strong violent intent when she says:

> Stun the sun, seek out his blood;
>   those faded energies
> go unravaged, and Time the droll troll
> crouches on your chest
>   dribbling.
>
> (*AL* 30)

However, the poet is conscious of the essential indifference with which the sun and the time go on, no matter what happens to whom. "Throw a spear at the Sun," or "sling a stone at the sun to bloody his eye", he "can't be killed." The tyranny of time hinted at here continues to engage Namjoshi's creative attention and comes in for a more elaborate treatment in some of her later work. The poet indulges in hypothetical reasoning and asks:

> But if the sun were mortal, then what would happen?
>
> (*AL* 32)

In an extraordinarily telling description she interprets the daily rising and daily setting of the sun as the daily dual between the sun and Death.

> That gay lancer, Death,
>   and his crony, the sun, joust every day.
>
> (*AL* 32)

In subsequent explorations, the poet realizes that death is 'not external' but comes from within. To die free and easy is, therefore, a kind of success and not surrender.

In this rather long exhortation on the theme of death, the

peroration clearly indicates the living should let the dead go. Employing the imagery of water world, Namjoshi suggests that the fish should be returned to the waters of the sea and not kept out by the stubborn child. The following lines reconcile the dilemma of the section: 'Discourse with the Dead' by nullifying the dichotomy between life and death, between sunrise and sunset, between meeting and parting.

> Consider now the giant father
> And his no less giant daughter
> wading in the sea. Do they leave
> or approach? Is that sunrise
> or sunset?
> Leave them to their occupation,
> they are happy enough,
> handsome enough, further beatitude
> left to otherhands, a farther future.
>
> (*AL* 38)

Namjoshi's poetic and philosophic preoccupations with the death of her father articulated in *The Authentic Lie* bring her professed ideological positioning as a feminist under interrogation. How does one reconcile the burden of anti-patriarchal protest recurring in her work with the emotional dependence on the father figure expressed in these verses? Namjoshi tries to clarify this ambivalence in her introduction to the section from *The Authentic Lie* in *Because of India*: "I loved my father, I also liked him for the child, for his daughter, his only crime was that he died. For the woman writing the poems, the central task was to clarify and shape the raw material of the grief of the child." She follows this up with a confession: "At the time I wasn't a feminist, in the sense that I had no understanding of patriarchy as an institution" (1989: 41).

The process of conversion was underway when she revised these poems for publication. She had come under the influence of lesbian/radical feminism; she was attracted by the revolutionary logic of their arguments and she was convinced of the need for asserting individual freedom in choosing one's own destiny. At the same time she had not yet viewed her newly developed ideological position in the context of her familial loyalties or social obligations. She was in fact not fully conscious of the political implications of the freedom she was questing for. This accounts for the contradictions and ambivalence one finds in these two anthologies of Namjoshi's poems written over a period of six to seven years and revised another three to four years later.

The second section entitled "Assassins" deals with death at a more abstract level. The killer and the killed, the eater and the eaten are after all two aspects of the same fact and every one and every being is an assassin in some sense or the other. The very first poem in this sequence "Exercise" gives us a clue to the paradoxical nature of the experience of death. Whether you struggle with yourself or you embrace yourself, both movements eventually lead to death. Death, decay and degeneration are natural processes, and they chart their own course unmindful of individual responses.

"Graven Images", one of the most richly complex poems in the section, shows how even the idols of God wear out slowly but splendidly over a period of time. The huge and heavy stone god is inert to stimuli, unmoved by action and is anthropomorphic. The stone god is impassive and inactive. Nothing can really induce him to act, not even his wife. If God could be moved, he might kill, but he cannot be made to act. But even this stone god is eroded in a slow process which might take thousands of years:

> Every night his godship recedes, inches
> into rock in the wind and rain.
> It will probably take him 6,000 years,
> 7,000 years, to alter his smile,

to erode his nose. Human beings
help, their stroking and petting,

their persistent kissing.
His priests rub him down
in butter every day.

(*AL* 43)

The title 'Assassins' comes from Namjoshi's logic that everything eventually gets killed and everyone of us is an assassin in some sense or the other. In fact this is not the first time she comes up with this view of life. As early as in her 1967 collection, she said:

We're constructed to kill
Whether we kill just sheep or men.

("Rationale" *MP* 31)

This notion is further deliberated upon and elaborated in *The Authentic Lie*. A series of poems under the title "The Graven Images" demonstrate Namjoshi's position that art, which is generally considered as something that immortalizes, actually 'freezes' life and thus assassinates. For instance, consider these lines:

Under a stone tree of which
the leaves are made of stone,
a man lies asleep. Even his lashes
are made of stone. Sometimes
an ant will cross an eyelid.
No muscle moves. This is a man
Who was probably *loved and thus preserved*.

(Italics mine *AL* 45)

Art, action, love – anything that is plastic and creative – turns life to stone, preserves, assassinates, stops altogether pulsations and creates a permanent state that is stiff in every joint and sinew, incapable of movement like the heavy stone god.

Whenever Namjoshi fails to understand the logic of human

interactions and experiences, she turns to nature and the animal world for parallel phenomena. Ant and ant trap become her images to probe the meaning of existence and death critically. Ants live as if "they were sexless" and work "non-stop", hardly ever sleeping, and perhaps never dreaming. Then the poet raises the question: "How about death?" There is ecstasy in their death and ease and comfort in their dissolution. The soul of the ant enters the ant trap, its body nature's scrap. There is a lesson one can learn from the experience of ants. The only aspiration worthwhile is aspiring "to be" (*AL* 52). "Minimal Murder" too is about the soft and soundless death of insects like spiders. Interestingly, the poet points out that every creature is both an agent and an effect in the chain of assassinations that occur in nature all the time. Whether we pluck a flower, walk on ants or spray an insecticide, we are playing our role as assassins in causing death.

The question that keeps coming back insistently in this discourse on death is: What is it like to die? What is the nature of life and death? (*AL* 57). Conceptualizing death is different from experiencing death. Death may be likened to a dream. Dream is neither true nor false: because it is a dream it is a lie, because it is experienced it is truth. Death like dream is an authentic lie.

Namjoshi cannot sustain a serious or a profound-sounding argument for too long. Irony and playful subversion are her forte and the readers of *The Authentic Lie* are only too happy when she resumes her usual style in the last couple of verses in this collection. 'The Rules, Regulations and Amenities of Hell' is a typical Namjoshi poem which ensures that conventional notions of hell are subverted and critiqued. Readers familiar with Dante's descriptions of Inferno and Miltons' graphic account of the sulphurous flames of hell, a dungeon horrible, find Namjoshi playing non-chalantly with all stereotypical images of hell in her version. For instance, in Namjoshi's hell "the compulsive scrubbers can burn and burn and are sure to be clean, for the everlasting fire consumes all." The rules and regulations of hell "merely ensure the liberties of hell." Furthermore,

> No madness in hell. You cannot go mad.
> No drugs in hell. You cannot forget.
> No death, decay or death in hell. You cannot die.
>
> (*AL* 63)

After all these clear inversions and revised descriptions of hell, Namjoshi concludes: "The landscape of hell is the body of man, not wide awake and not quite dead." (AL 63) Thus the poet constantly straddles simultaneously the two worlds of the serious, and the comic, the sacred and the profane, the spiritual and the mundane, blurring all lines of demarcation.

Works Cited

Daly, Mary. *Gyn/Ecology: The Metaethics of Radical Feminism*. Boston: Beacon Press, 1978.

Halliday, Caroline. "The Naked Majesty of God: Contemporary Lesbian Erotic Poetry." *Lesbian and Gay Writing*. Ed. Mark Lilly. London: Macmillan, 1990.

Namjoshi, Suniti. *The Jackass and the Lady*. Calcutta: Writers Workshop, 1980.

—. *The Authentic Lie*. Frederiction, Canada: Fiddlehead, 1982.

—. *Because of India: Selected Poems*. London: Onlywomen Press, 1989.

Phelan, Shane. *Identity Politics: Lesbianism and the Limits of Community*. Philadelphia: Temple University Press, 1989.

Simon, Sherry. Review of *Feminist Fables: The Literary Criterion*, 20.1 (1985): 264-67.

4

Revisionist Mythmaking: *Feminist Fables* and *From the Bedside Book of Nightmares*

Namjoshi's most successful work to date *Feminist Fables* clearly spells out her ideological position as a radical feminist. This book comes immediately after her complete conversion to her new faith and sets down her agenda as a feminist. Namjoshi gives a detailed account of the circumstances that led to her ideological conversion in the introduction to the section from *Feminist Fables* in *Because of India*.

Namjoshi took her first sabbatical in 1978-79 and spent nearly fourteen months in England. She came into contact with lesbian and gay groups and got to understand their philosophy of life. This exposure initially unsettled her. It was through her association with Christine Donald that she came to grips with the complexity of radical feminist thought and movement. Moving closely with Christine Donald, who bravely wore the badges of feminism and gay liberation despite the aggressive responses of the society around her, was a kind of education for Namjoshi. This marked a phase of political awakening for her. As she herself explains "It shamed me that I was letting other women do the fighting for me." She therefore came out openly in print and press to clarify her ideological position as a lesbian feminist and thus joined the activist groups. During her sabbatical, she had read Kate Millet, Adrienne Rich and other important feminist writers of the time and her own work that followed became a part of her committed struggle for the realization of gender justice.

The feminist movement entered a new phase in the 1970's when Radicalesbians came out with their manifesto called "The Woman-Identified Woman" and opened up new ground for a discourse about and understanding of lesbianism. This document defined the position of a lesbian as follows:

> A lesbian is the rage of all women condensed to the point of explosion. She is the woman who, often beginning at an extremely early age, acts in accordance with her inner compulsion to be a more complete and freer human being than her society – perhaps then, but certainly later -- cares to allow her. These needs and actions, over a period of years, bring her into painful conflict with people, situations, the accepted ways of thinking, feeling and behaving until she is in a state of continual war with everything around her, and usually with herself. She may not be fully conscious of the political implications of what for her began as personal necessity, but on some level she has not been able to accept the limitations and oppression laid on her by the most basic role of her society – the female role..... To the extent that she cannot expel the heavy socialization that goes with being female, she can never truly find peace with herself. For she is caught somewhere between accepting society's views of her – in which case she cannot accept herself -- and coming to understand

> what this sexist society has done to her and why it is functional and necessary for it to do so.
>
> (1973: 240-41)

These arguments of Radicalesbians brought into focus the need for political unity among feminists and stressed that the basic structure of control over women is that of sexuality and in particular the requirement of heterosexuality. It is important to reject this structure if women are to become whole beings. Namjoshi's work beginning with *Feminist Fables* draws on these various developments in lesbian/feminist thought.

Namjoshi's re-writing of fables in *Feminist Fables*, and of canonical texts such as *The Tempest*, and the classical myths of Perseus and Andromeda, Penelope, Antigone etc. in *The Bedside Book of Nightmares* may best be read as a part of feminist mythmaking, or to be more precise, feminist re-visionist mythmaking. Like all radical groups feminists/lesbians incorporate myths. Myths are, to recall Mircia Eliade's oft quoted definition, "sacred stories" that "illustrate what primarily concerns [a] society ... and help to explain certain features in that society's religion, laws, social structure, environment, history or cosmology" (1963: 6). In any culture, these myths have come to embody patriarchal perspectives because all social and cultural institutions – religion, law, history and so on – have been largely under the control of men. Viewed thus mythology should appear an inhospitable terrain for a woman writer. In the world of myths we find conquering gods and heroes, loathful dragons and damsels in distress. Women portrayed here are either sexually wicked seducers such as Circe, Helen, Medusa and Eve or virtually impassive angels like Mary, Alcestice and Cinderella. It is thanks to myth that we believe women must be either monsters or angels (de Beauvoir 1968: 157-223). Myths create stereotypical subject positions for women. The good women, the heroines are invariably beautiful, passive and powerless while female characters who are powerful are often evil, ugly and ill-tempered. "Being powerful is mainly associated with being unwomanly" (Zipes 1986: 197).

Women writers, however, do not abandon myths all together in their literary writing. The need for myth of some sort appears to be ineradicable. Kate Millet reworks the myth of Persephone – Demeter in her *Sita* (1976); Monique Wittig fabulates lesbian myth of origins as against the Genesis story in *Les Guérillers* (1971); Adrienne Rich in "Diving into the Wreck" carries with her "a book of myths ... in which/our names do not appear" and declares that she seeks "the wreck and not the story of the wreck/the thing itself and not the myth" thus implying that it is important for a woman to go to the crux of the myth in order to dis-cover the truth. In all these cases, women writers are engaged in what may be called "re-visionist myth making."

In her theoretical essay, "When We Dead Awaken: Writing as Re-Vision," Adrienne Rich stresses the importance of re-writing old stories and myths from a female perspective in the feminist cognitive revolution. In retelling myths, women above all re-constitute the worlds contained in words and offer correctives to the male biased versions of words as well as worlds. She explains the objectives of this re-visionist project as follows:

> Re-vision -- the act of looking back, of seeing with fresh eyes, of entering an old text from a new critical direction – is for us more than a chapter in cultural history: it is an act of survival. Until we can understand the assumptions in which we are drenched we cannot know ourselves. And this drive to self-knowledge, for woman, is more than a search for identity: it is part of her refusal of the self-destructiveness of male-dominated society.
>
> (1975: 90)

Retelling an old tale from a fresh perspective, reordering the world contained in it according to a woman's perceptions, rectifying the value systems projected in the past to ensure gender-justice, liberating woman from the stereotypes of stories of the past -- these are the objectives of re-visionist myth making. This is an overtly political project aimed at overturning the patriarchal domination of culture and language. In lesbian myth-making, this project gains an additional edge of urgency since it is an important aspect of their attempt to create a lesbian identity and culture. It is interesting to recall here what one of the characters in Noretta Koertge's *Valley of the Amazon* (1984), Helen, says of the power of myths: "Don't ever doubt the power of myths... – I mean women's myths, not the bullshit stories we grew up with. We have to build a feminist mythology and recover woman's herstory" (38).

To create new stories and myths, feminist writers draw upon many of the fundamental myths and symbols found in patriarchal culture – myth of origins, the quest, the fall from innocence, the witch, the dragon, the island. They skilfully and imaginatively blend ancient myth and prehistory with contemporary feminist ideology and create a tradition of female literary heritage. However, like the myths of patriarchy, re-visionist myths of women writers are not static. They have been continually questioned and revised in version after version because transformation is the essence of this movement of re-visionist myth making.

Namjoshi's *Feminist Fables* and *From the Bedside Book of Nightmares* exemplify all the essential features of re-visionist myth making and what follows is a reading of these two texts in the light of the foregoing theoretical positions.

* * *

Feminist Fables is a collection of ninety-nine stories dealing with a range of women's issues from a feminist perspective. Namjoshi makes clever use of Anderson's tales, *Panchatantra* stories, Aesops fables and other texts as intertexts to deconstruct the patriarchal world order securely ensconced in these seemingly innocent stories on which generations of children are raised. Even nursery rhymes and songs are re-viewed here from a feminist perspective and the result is astounding. No form of knowledge, no scrap of writing, no act of narration is free from guilt of complicity in promoting the hegemony of the male. The issues raised in these fables are of course basic to the human condition: Intimacy, loneliness, death, anger, ambition and desire; and these thread their way through this collection and are explored now with an eye for the comic, for the absurd, now with a sense of poignant sadness and longing.

Namjoshi's fables effect a cognitive revolution featuring startling heroines, inverting some popularly known tales of the past, interrogating conventional systems of thought and morality and forging alternative perspectives of looking at life and experience. Evoking fun and mirth, however, is central to her fabulation. The first story in this collection, "From the Panchtantra", sets the tone for her re-visionist project. A poor brahmin in the holy city of Banares prays to Lord Vishnu for a son. God, out of absentmindedness or for some other more obstruse reason, blesses (or curses?) him with a daughter. The disappointed brahmin makes the best of the situation by teaching his daughter what he knew. "Though only a woman she was a brahmin, so she learned very fast...." (*FF* 1). The father and daughter both meditate and Lord Vishnu promptly appears again. The brahmin quickly reiterates his plea for a son and the Lord says: "Next time around." The brahmin in his next birth becomes a woman and bears eight sons. Is it a boon or a curse? The brahmin girl simply asks for human status but Lord Vishnu knows it is not easy to grant human status to females and so wriggles out of the difficult situation by appointing a committee. Namjoshi ironizes caste as well as gender hegemony and exposes the discriminatory practices which condemn certain classes, castes and sections of society to an inferior status. Gods too are a party to this discrimination!

In another tale, 'The Gods,' a childless couple is blessed with a daughter. They pray to the gods every morning and evening seeking divine grace for their child. The child, with the blessings of gods and parents, grows up to be a really remarkable woman. She could run faster than any one else in the village; she excelled in studies; sang well and impressed everybody. But all this cannot set right the original problem with her. She is a woman and "To be sodamned good," after all is "not womanly" (*FF* 37). The writer thus brings all traditional expectations of femininity under interrogation.

The little princes in the story of the same title is more accomplished than her brother in every way. She passes all tests, hunting, drinking, tennis and mathematics. The king disappointed with his son lets the daughter rule. But "Fortunately the citizens had more sense." They brought the prince back to power and thus was order restored. The ironic closure raises questions about concepts such as order, chaos and restoration and proves that these are all constructs developed and maintained only to keep the male power in tact.

There are a number of stories in this collection which directly address the issue of lesbianism. "The Badge-wearing Dyke and Her two Maiden Aunts," for instance, makes the point that woman's love for woman is as old as creation itself. In this story, two elderly spinster mice live together unmindful of the political implications of their personal relationships. A university-educated niece comes to visit, and she wears badges of Gay Liberation and Lesbian solidarity. When she discovers that her aunts have always practised what she has taken to preaching, she surrenders to their conviction. The story clearly suggests that woman's love for woman is both natural and quite ancient. The ironic tone employed by the narrator registers a strong protest against the conventional gender roles and norms which have always strategically reduced woman to an inferior position in social, intellectual and cultural terms. In a number of tales Namjoshi strongly revolts against the definitions of 'woman' allowed by the patriarchal tradition. For instance, "A Moral Tale" demonstrates the social antagonism to lesbian love relationship. When a female beast loves Beauty, it is considered monstrous and she becomes an object of ridicule. Books, stories and society all collide in upholding the virtue of heterosexuality in which "men loved women, and women loved men, and men rode off and had all sorts of adventures and women stayed at home," (*FF* 23). The Beast pays for its strange affections: It lives and dies lonely. "Happy Ending", on the other hand, has a different closure. Drakes and ducks are permitted to like their own kind and live happily ever after. There were women who desired one another long before the crucial nomenclature for lebianism actually appeared. Reconceptualization of the normal makes lesbian existence possible and even desirable. Namjoshi suggests that heterosexuality is not the only way to live and might not always be the best way to live.

"I See You What You Are" is an ironic re-writing of the story of friendship between Viola disguised as a page and the love-lorn Olivia. Namjoshi charges the scene with lesbian possibilities and asks "would that have been wrong?" (*FF* 91). There are other stories such as "Friends", "The Homicidal Streak", "Troglodyte" which stress the naturalness of intimacy between women. Namjoshi's attempts to inscribe lesbian desire in her stories and thus demolish the heterosexual hegemony is clearly political.

Namjoshi retells some of the familiar tales such as "The Red Ridinghood", "Hansel and Gretel", "The Princess and the Pea", "The Ugly Duckling", "Cinderella", "Perseus and Andromeda", from an essentially woman's point of view. Even as she uses these tales as intertexts, it is the androcentric culture that she actually takes up for a critical consideration. Namjoshi retells these tales with slight but careful slippages, and gives them a subtly subversive twist which practically makes them stand on head, and lays open an unreasonably biased social order contained with in them. For instance, Namjoshi's little

Red Ridinghood makes a new connection between the wolf and the forester! Gretel stays with the witch, while Hansel runs home scared; little princess wears men's clothes and challenges her brother to a fight; ugly duckling is not really ugly but a swan among ducklings; Cinderella does not live happily ever after but gets separated from her handsome husband; Eve makes paradise where she walks and there are several such delightfully shocking subversions which invent an emancipatory relation to the dominant discourse.

"The Princess and the Pea" tale in Namjoshi's narrative does not end with the establishment of the authenticity of the Princess's identity. Instead, it begins there and gives a new twist to the story of the genuine princess whose sleep gets disturbed because of a small green pea under seven soft cushioned beds. The genuine princess is so sensitive that she cannot see the sick or the ugly. The whole town is proud of their genuine princess. At this point, Namjoshi effects a clever reversal in the narrative: "but it soon became obvious that her skin was such that she was allergic to everything." (*FF* 5), and finally the genuine princess catches a cold and dies of it. The writer makes the reader see the absurdity of the original narrative through her re-visionist re-reading.

Subversion in Namjoshi's text is not mere substitution of woman in man's place but an imaginary rewriting of the text and reconstitution of the context. For instance, in the original Perseus and Andromeda myth Perseus fights the monster to save the helpless princess. In Namjoshi's version, Andromeda asks for a change of roles, she opts to turn into the monster and then runs away with the monster turned into prince leaving the prince/princess in the lurch. The author shows that the wicked monster, like the damsel in distress, is also a construct of the patriarchal master narrative. She liberates both the princess and the dragon from the constraints of conventional constructs.

Sometimes Namjoshi extends a familiar tale beyond the conventional ending and allows it to describe unconventional developments. Namjoshi dismisses the comfortable ending: "they lived happily ever after" and replaces it with the insistent interrogation: "then what happened?" For instance, she re-writes the familiar Cinderella tale thus:

> The Prince married Cinderella (It pays to have such very small feet.) But soon they started squabbling 'You married me for my money,' was the Prince's charge. 'You married me for my looks,' was C's reply. 'But your looks will fade, where as my money will last. Not a fair bargain'. 'No', said Cinderella and simply walked out.
>
> AND THEN WHAT HAPPENED?
>
> (*FF* 112)

The question upsets the assumptions of the conventional happy ending forging the quotidian reality of monitory transactions in the fabular world of fantasy. Namjoshi's feminist rendering of the familiar tales successfully lays open the underlying patriarchal designs. In "Runner", Namjoshi asks why a beautiful princess like Atlanta should allow herself to be distracted by golden apples. Even if the apples were to be taken as symbolic, the story still would make no sense. Atlanta, the author reasons, was healthy and needed no apples; she was wealthy and did not need gold; was acclaimed a beautiful princess and did not need to face any more tests. Then the whole story must have been the fabrication of a vicious male imagination. Again, in Namjoshi's version of "The Emperor's New Clothes", a little girl takes off her clothes, emulating the emperor, but her mother promptly advises her, "Don't be silly, darling. Only little boys grow up to be emperors. As for little girls, they marry Emperors; and they learn to hold their tongues, particularly on the subject of the Emperor's clothes" (*FF* 8), exposing the discriminatory practices in the patriarchal world.

Even as Namjoshi strongly urges the need for a cognitive overhaul and a revolutionary transformation of the existing world order and moral universe, she is practical enough to see that such a change is not easy to accomplish. "The Loathly Lady" is a satire on the lip service paid to women's issues in political world. Queen Guinevere with the permission of King Arthur decides to take up the "Woman's Question". She looks at her ladies for volunteers. But there are no enthusiasts among women. The king sends a knight who comes back with a loathly lady. The loathly lady is changed into a beautiful woman overnight, and every one is content that the Woman's Question has been satisfactorily tackled. Again, the "Incredible Woman" in the story, "Broadcast Alive" rages through the skies, lassoes a planet, rescues a starship and accomplishes many such heroic tasks but then "takes time off to visit her psychiatrist" since "she is at heart a really womanly woman and all she wants is a normal life" (*FF* 63). The question here is "what is the norm and who made these norms?" Unless these gender norms are questioned and demolished, liberation of women remains a myth. In "Her Mother's Daughter" the mother refuses to see the point in her feminist daughter's argument that women had all along been relegated to a secondary position in the man-made world. In fact she believes: 'that's how it should be' (*FF* 96). To her surprise, Namjoshi finds that most women are willing victims of the patriarchal system. They don't seem to see the millstone around their necks!

Namjoshi's feminist re-readings and re-writings of old fables accomplish two complementary things: they appropriate positive but male-oriented symbols by feminizing them and they renew negative female-associated symbols by endowing them with positive value. Generally, all negative women characters fall into two categories – wayward girls or wicked witches. To be a wayward girl usually has something to do with pre-marital sex, to be a wicked woman has something to do with adultery. Namjoshi's stories invoke both these stereotypes to demolish them, and expose the underlying unjust assumptions. For instance, in "Nymph" Namjoshi gives three versions of the story of Daphne. Whether God chases Daphne or Daphne chases god, it is Daphne who is turned into a green laurel. This is so because as Namjoshi ironically adds: "That's what happens to ungrateful women." "Signpost" is a powerful critique of all tales about wicked witches. The story goes thus:

> So the witch having understood at last that her amazing powers were wanted by no one, of no consequence, and in all probability likely to alarm, turned into a tree. She never sprouted leaves, never grew flowers. In effect she was dead. Her life had been useless. But in her death she was useful. Disguised though she was, the townsfolk knew her. They pointed her out to precocious little girls as a clear example of what is it that happens.
>
> (*FF* 97)

Witches and wicked women are signposts erected by patriarchy to scare young girls into conformity with norms laid down by the male world.

It is important to note that none of the characters in Namjoshi's stories have individuating names. They are given descriptive names like "The Princess", "The Ugly One", "The Loathly Lady", "She-monster" "Bird Woman", "Green Slave Woman" etc. The purpose is obvious: the author means to give her characters a representative identity, and she intends to raise issues that are of relevance to the entire female community. These women are depicted as representatives of something more than individual characters: they are wayward girls and wicked women, princesses and slaves; mothers and daughters; nymphs and wicked witches. All of them are restless with the identities culture has imposed on them, and are out to cast away their traditional roles and launch into the world on their own terms. What Namjoshi achieves by setting free these women from the prison house of old tales is the liberation of the readers from the tyranny of stereotypical images. Feminist tales in this collection are told in a complicated voice: incisively ironic, unmistakably didactic yet delightful witty and engaging. All these stories underscore a moral: there is need to break all kinds of conditioning, above all cognitive conditioning in order to be able to apprehend the possibility of gender justice. Namjoshi projects this moral indirectly and subtly by teaching through example.

Structually Namjoshi's tales draw on the *Panchatantra*, Aesops Fables and the Jataka tales. Using both prose and verse in the narrative unmindful of generic distinction is an important feature of fabular literature. Besides, fables freely employ epigrammatic verses often drawn from sacred texts of the past. These maxims blend wisdom with wit, instructing and entertaining the readers simultaneously. Namjoshi retains these stylistic features of fabular literature in her rewriting of the tales from the past.

A note on Namjoshi's use of the 'fable' form is in order here. The fable is said to be a performative utterance and has been fundamentally moralistic in intent. Historians have suggested that tail piece of the moral is actually prior to the tale itself, which is then created to illustrate the aphorism. The morals that fables preach belong to a patriarchal order and demand implicit conformity. How does Namjoshi employ this pithy, epigrammatic form of the fable in the cause of contemporary feminism? Namjoshi turns fables into a sort of counter discourse and creates an occasion for provocation and questioning. She designs new morals for new times and demands that every thing including thinking itself need to be rethought. The short and cryptic form of fable proves an effective tool for articulating revolutionary ideas.

Generally, fables and fairy tales are so constructed that their reading position is passive. The reader here (who is often a child) becomes a passive receiver of events, and the narrative makes no demand that he/she participate in any kind of interpretation. "Things 'happen,' 'are done to' protagonists, told to the reader, from a position of omniscience and authority, making the reader unquestioningly" passive (Jackson

1981: 154). Fairy tales thus exemplify a conservative ideological discourse. But when feminists rewrite these stories, they implore the readers to actively re-evaluate the nature of fantasies represented in these apparently harmless and value-neutral tales meant for childhood amusement, and urge them to participate in the process of meaning-making.

Each of the stories retold by Namjoshi stirs the reader to probe the familiar tales and discover the underlying hegemonic designs. In these stories the reader simultaneously sees two versions of the narrative – the revised version and its discursive referent i.e., the traditional narrative. This enables the reader to engage in a continual comparison between the text on the printed page and its absent referent. From the comprehension of the difference arises an awareness of the discriminatory politics underlying the so called innocent and value-free literature meant for a child reader.

Sherry Simon in her review of Namjoshi's work remarks: "In the fables particularly there is an unresolved tension between timeliness and atemporality, authorial implication and detachment. But these contradictions have been, and will hopefully continue to be, fruitful" (1985: 267). It is Namjoshi's method to speak in paradoxes, play with oppositions and continually erect and demolish polarities.

* * *

In *From the Bedside Book of Nightmares*, her next book, Namjoshi continues to rewrite old texts, but the focus now shifts to the canonical texts of European and British literature. The narrators voice turns sharper and angrier in this volume.

The Bedside Book of Nightmares is Namjoshi's most violent work, and in these verses the poet confronts rather squarely some of the inner most conflicts that trouble her. She explores the implications of gay liberation and women's liberation for familial relationships and attachments. How does a warring woman who seeks freedom from all bonds of patriarchy – paternal as well as marital – look at family loyalties? How does a feminist/lesbian view herself vis-à-vis the world around her? Namjoshi is actually evaluating her own political ideology against her commitment and loyalty to family relationships in these verses.

The book is divided into three sections: "From Baby F" focuses on Baby Frankenstein's submissions to her mother; "The Creature" deals with Namjoshi's favourite theme of politics of representation, and "The Snapshots of Caliban" offers musings of a female Caliban and holds an interrogatory relationship with the original canonical text: Shakespeare's *The Tempest*.

One of the most important moments in a lesbian's evolution is the moment of open declaration of her lesbianism to her own mother. This confrontation with one's mother, wrought with much pain and agony, is a significant aspect of lesbian experience. No wonder a great deal of lesbian writing features this trauma and its repercussions. Why do lesbian daughters fear that coming out will bring rejection and abandonment from their mothers? Why do mothers fear and despise their daughters' lesbianism?

Looking at the mother-daughter relationship and a host of psychological issues attendant upon this relationship as it operates within the structure of patriarchy and compulsory heterosexuality, one can conclude that it is the appropriation of woman into her husband's patriarchal family that effects a separation between mother and daughter. Unlike the heterosexual daughter, the lesbian daughter retains or reclaims the mother-daughter bond, paying no homage to male domination or ownership of her body. In *Of Woman Born: Motherhood as Experience and Institution*, Adrienne Rich notes the intimacy of mother-daughter relationship thus:

> This Cathexis between mother and daughter – essential, distorted, misused – is the great unwritten story. Probably there is nothing in human nature more resonant with charges than the

> flow of energy between two biologically alike bodies, one of which has lain in amniotic bliss inside the other, one of which has labored to give birth to the other. The materials are here for the deepest mutuality and the most painful estrangement. Yet this relationship has been minimized and trivialized in the annals of patriarchy .... Like intense relationships of women in general, the relationship between mother and daughter has been profoundly threatening to men.
>
> (1976: 226-27)

A great deal of feminist writing, therefore, explores this important relationship and tries to restore the primacy of matrilineage. This relationship acquires an extra edge of intensity in lesbian writing.

Namjoshi chooses Baby Frankenstein as her mouthpiece to articulate her feelings towards her mother. Frankenstein, who conceives the grandiose notion of creating life from the inanimate, galvanizes into life a misshapen and ugly creature endowed with supernatural strength. The creature is excluded from human society, but it has very human needs and emotions and acquires a lofty education from books. Frankenstein tries all means to tame the monster he has created, but eventually gets killed by his own creature.

Namjoshi turns Mary Shelley's Frankensteinian creature into a female child -- Baby F -- and uses the child as her mouthpiece to articulate her own feelings as a lesbian daughter. After all, Frankenstein's monster is no horror in itself but becomes horrid in the scheme of popular perceptions. The very first verse in this collection establishes a devouring relationship between the mother and daughter. The persona says:

> It might have been simpler, mother,
> if you had found me in a cabbage patch,
> green and round and exceeding healthy.
> Then you could have eaten me.
> Or if I had been a caterpillar

And you had been a leaf.

(*FBB* 7)

The creator and the creature, the mother and the offspring in hunger for each other long to possess and repossess each other. Namjoshi recalls in sensitive verse, mother's joy at mothering, finding her own flesh take shape and life. Mother feels the joy of giving birth, but what does the baby feel?

You are glad that I was born.
I cannot remember what the baby feels.

(*FBB* 9)

Mother's dreams for her child and the child's dreams for herself may not always coincide; perhaps, more often, they don't. While the mother hopes to see her child grow into a gentle, kind and lovely young lady, demure and docile, the daughter may grow up resisting this image. It is useful to recall Mary Daly's incisive analysis of Mary Shelley's work in this context:

Mary Shelley displayed prophetic insight when
she wrote *Frankenstein* foretelling the technological
father's fusion of male mother-miming and necrophilia
in a boundary violation that ultimately points toward
the total elimination of women.

(1979: 70).

Dr. Frankenstein in Mary Shelley's work expresses a bizarre necrophilic "maternal instinct" in making the monster whom he later repudiated, fled from in terror and destroyed by in agony.

The mother nurtures silently serious fears about her Frankensteinean child. The anxiety, apprehension and panic the mother of a weird daughter experiences grow inside her like a mountain. The daughter here confesses:

They told me you were brave and rode horses
with an extreme recklessness.
When still very little

I grew up thinking that I was also brave.
    But of your fear,
of how it grew inside you and sat there

like a mountain, I know nothing at all.

(*FBB* 11)

Then Namjoshi sets out to explore the relevance of maternal ancestry in the life of a woman. The family history records the male lineage where the females serve as mere appendages. The Female Gulliver of Namjoshi searches for her female ancestors in the island of the Sorceress. But the faces that appear look unfamiliar and this act of recalling female ancestors causes worry to ancestors themselves. Re-membering ancient bonds with women of the past is a necessary first step in female bonding. The thrust of this section which articulates a woman's quest for a female tradition is best captured in the following lines:

We loved those kindly gentlemen, I mean
your own father, and your daughter's father.
But in our long ancestry,
    where are the women?

(*FBB* 13)

The lesbian daughter embodies the spirit of the matrilineage much more than her heterosexual sisters who are given away by fathers to husbands in bonds of matrimony.

The traditional familial structures enforce an estrangement between mother and daughter and force the latter to identify herself with the more powerful parent – the father.

The kindly king sat on his throne.
    He was secure.
The king's daughter sat on his lap.
    She was very secure.

(*FBB* 16)

But this security is, after all, an illusion and it is often too late to change ones loyalties. Baby F loves and hates intensely, and she is savagely critical of the social institutions that have demanded girls and women to be self-effacing. She refuses to be another faceless nameless female, and insists that the family saga be re-written from a woman's point of view.

Namjoshi also looks at gender discrimination that subtly operates in child-rearing in a patriarchal society. In the verse quoted below, the girl child complains of being marginalized in a male dominated familial structure, and holds her mother responsible not so much for her loss, as for not tutoring her to lose.

> You eventually produced one human being
> who was very like me
> He thought of his father and his father's father
> I thought of my mother and my mother's mother
> It seems almost natural that we frequently fought.
> But it was not natural. He was carefully tutored
> You didn't make it clear that I ought to have lost.
>
> (*FBB* 19)

The female child, thus marginalized, invents her own vicious ways of finding small gains. The persona in "Confession" tells us how she made her younger brother believe that the latter had 'bright green hair' and felt thrilled at having fooled him.

"Snow White and Rose Green" is Namjoshi's version of the story of two sisters. In fact there are innumerable stories about two sisters in all literatures. In these traditional tales one is a good girl and the other bad. In Namjoshi's tale of two sisters each is very different from the other. But these two sisters loved one another and this made their mother unhappy. They try everything within their means including surgically re-forming themselves into one all-virtuous and the other all-evil creatures just to please her. Nothing satisfies their mother because they are still two, and they still love each other. The writer ironically points out at the mother's discomfiture at her daughters' lesbian proclivities. "Try lies, mother?" is an interesting short narrative which proposes various models for mother-daughter relationship. With twenty years distance between them how can they become contemporaries? In one alternative they go fishing, the child catches fish, the mother tells her the story of fisher king and they fry and eat fish. In the second alternative, there is still the same twenty years gap, the mother is an able pilot and the child feels proud of her mother's strength. In the third, the father and his friends hold guns and go gaming while the two women, mother and daughter, are left out of the game of hunting. In the fourth, they all turn into crocodiles and live happily ever after. Animals live happily since they are not divided in the name of civilization or social order.

One of the dominant themes in this section of the poem is how mother as creator finds her daughter – her own creature – a Frankenstein monster. Yet a strange love-hate relationship exists between them. The mother despite housing the unborn child for nine months, despite rearing her for nineteen years does not really produce the finished product. The child then grows up independently sometimes shattering the fond images of an ideal daughter nurtured by her mother.

The second section "Creature" further focuses on the relationship between the creator and the creature. This section abounds in images of violence and the recurring motif in this section is seeking of freedom at all costs. This section begins with a reference to the frenzy of Maenads. Maenadism enabled women to leave their homes, mingle with their sisters and assert their individual desire, joy and ecstasy. Namjoshi finds an apt metaphor for lesbian emotions in the ritual of Maenads, and she subtly points out that women's resistance to the power of patriarchy is neither new nor recent. Maenadic ritual had always strongly stimulated mythical imagination. For instance, *Bacchae of Euripides* shows us women who tear animals apart, handle snakes, eat raw meat and are vulnerable to iron and fire. In invoking Maenads, Namjoshi is actually retrieving the tradition of female revolt and action. The persona here says:

> The maenads beat my grandfather to death.
> And my brother, he was caught too,
> caught like a rabbit in the thorn forest.
> They said I did it,
> that I licked the blood and ate rabbit flesh.
> But I didn't do it
> I remember. I was a witness.

(*FBB* 33)

Another theme that Namjoshi often returns to in her creative work is the silencing of female voice. For instance, "Nasty Story" tells us how female presence was systematically marginalized and minimized in the name of civilization. Namjoshi also shows how the suffering and sorrow of women have always been totally ignored. The persona in one of her verses asks: "why are all the broken children boys?" and wonders if the girls do not suffer. The poem ends with the ironic observation:

> They (the girls) are the stones
> or the weather.

(*FBB* 34)

Namjoshi thematizes her own transformation from an ideal English literature student "with a centre of consciousness/so indisputably human" into "a little villainous creature" (35), who refuses to comply and indulges in vociferous protests. The poet further states her own difference from the majority of other women in terms of love and sexual identity, when she says:

> I wonder what those others
> – those lovers of men – do?

(*FBB* 37)

In "Call it a Process" Namjoshi comes down heavily on the exploitation of female body in the name of compulsory heterosexual relationships. To her, sex that is compulsory is worse than a murderous act. "Creature" attempts a more inclusive analysis of homosexual and heterosexual love relationships. The primal bonds among mothers, sisters, daughters and female friends are the soil from which lesbianism grows. But the patriarchal social order and familial structures have successfully come up with norms that shattered this natural bond, and consequently opting for a lesbian relationship has been marked as deviant behaviour. All women are creatures within this system and find it hard to move out of the compulsions and restrictions imposed by the so called 'normative behaviour'. In 'The Creature' the persona begins by talking about the intimacy she had developed with a woman who too reciprocated her friendship and love. There is a sudden break of this bond which is announced thus:

> But then he appeared,
> She looked up and laughed
> He looked down and smiled –
> from a monstrous height
> I skittered off fast
> Then I came back
> And watched them at it.
>
> (*FBB* 45)

The poet deliberately keeps the identity of the creature ambiguous and the descriptive words such as "I licked her throat" "I skittered off fast", "I came out of the bushes" suggest the creature could be a snake and invoke the imagery of Eden and the story of Eve, the archetypal woman.

In this section, several voices from old texts come alive to articulate their views. They refuse to keep to the original images given to them by their authors and declare their autonomy. Antigone in classical mythology breaks the edict of the king and buries her brother's corpse incurring royal wrath.

The reformed Antigone in Namjoshi's poem decides to save her own life rather than bury her brother and get into problems. Penelope weaves her interminable web not out of love or duty towards her husband but out of "a rage." After all "Virtuous women punish themselves." (*FBB* 39)

The last poem in this section, "The Fur Seals as Shown On Television" is a serious indictment of sexism that operates in all forms of popular representation including the electronic media. In the television show on seals, the beachmaster says of the female seal "... females are seldom,/if ever hurt," and hits it on the head. The seal goes down and nothing else is shown. While the T.V. announcer is excited about the show, the person watching it feels bruised and her head hurts. The television show on Fur seals only bears out the general insensitivity to the pain and hurt of the female kind. The so called entertainment also helps in circulating and popularizing stereotypical images and ideas which are charged with sexist assumptions.

The third and final sequence of the text, "Snapshots of Caliban" attempts a critical revaluation of power politics and combating egos by re-writing Shakespeare's *The Tempest*, the paradigmatic text of colonial relationships. There have been several re-writings of *The Tempest* in postcolonial literatures. Caliban has been appropriated as a powerful symbol of anticolonial resistance in postcolonial writing. Caliban, according to George Lamming, "is the excluded, that which is eternally below possibility... He is seen as an occasion, a state of existence which can be appropriated and exploited to the purposes of another's own development" (1984: 107). Postcolonial re-writings of *The Tempest* explode Prospero's old myth and show that Caliban has a history of his own, the history that may be seen as an aspect of the history of all subjugated men and women. Each reinscription of *The Tempest* is a local version of the old grand story invigorated and inflected by the revolutionary needs of the place and time. The feminist agenda is fundamental to Namjoshi's rewriting of the story of Caliban.

"Snapshots" is set in the island of Sycorax and the characters from Shakespeare's *The Tempest* are resurrected under their original names with one significant difference: Caliban is female and literate. She keeps a journal and jots down her responses albeit in a childlike language. *The Tempest* story is presented in a series of snapshots, and the imagery of photography dominates the text's structural ordering. The reader is left free to fill in the gaps and make connections between the various snapshots. The identity of the speaker remains unclear but the narrator does not exercise monopoly over the tale, allows several voices to emerge as excerpts from Caliban's notebook, Miranda's diary, and Prospero's meditation occupy a lot of narrative space minimizing the viewpoint of the omniscient narrator.

The opening statement hints at the major concern of this section: articulating the silent rage of the oppressed. Moving from alienation to revolution, from a recognition of injustice to resistance and articulation of rage is an important first step in any movement for autonomy. The narrator summons Caliban from the canonical texts: "She was squat and ugly./Sometimes she cried. Sometime she lied/She was so shy and sometimes so forthright/she disgusted me" (*FBB* 54). But the little Caliban resists the monstrous intentions of the narrator "trying to save herself/and me from me" (*FBB* 54). In a swift re-visionist step the narrator imagines Caliban in her natural chores: "Sleeping/her lips half-smiling," "absorbed in her dear dream" 'fishing/in a cranny of the island'. The hatred and disgust for Caliban evoked by the stereotype disappears and the narrator feels like approaching her slowly "to make friends." (*FBB* 55)

In the next snap Caliban and Miranda are both seen as little children fighting over sandcastles outside Prospero's cave. The sage comes out and finds the children happy. With a curled lip he withdraws,

> to brood once again on the storms
> he will cause, the tempest he'll make.
>
> (*FBB* 56)

Prospero right away appears as the arch manipulator who thrives by creating tempests and storms.

Caliban in her journal notes copiously her experience of discrimination, humiliation and exploitation. When Ferdinand chops trees and carries logs for one day, Miranda pities him. But Caliban has slogged for twelve years, and Miranda has shown no pity. Caliban notes:

> "They are playing chess I could learn too, I am not stupid. But they say it's a game intended for two. They have left me out".
>
> (*FBB* 57)

Caliban is, of course, not "stupid" and can see through the manipulations of cunning Prospero and his crew. In fact, Caliban is conscious of her knowledge of the native land which she imparted to the alien who through fraud and trickery ousted her from the possession of the land. She therefore argues: "These berries are nice, those are not nice. This water is fresh. That water is salt. I learnt. I learnt all that all by myself, and I told it to them. They were so pleased. But one day when I said to myself, 'Miranda is nice', and told it to her, she didn't like it. She told it to him. I was whipped afterwards" (*FBB* 57). As Caliban begins to see the deceit of the so called god-like men she ceases to trust them. She expresses her confidence in her own power to create and control when she puts down in her journal: "Soon, very soon. I shall people this island (with nice people)" (*FBB* 58).

The poem sequence, though titled "Snapshots of Caliban", directs the readers' attention equally on Miranda. There are excerpts from M's Journal too. Miranda's version too is important since Miranda symbolizes a popular female stereotype in male writing -- the virtuous angel. Miranda has a strange love-hate feeling for Caliban, she notes in her journal:

"Caliban is ill. I can't help wondering if she is going to die. I do not want her to die. I am surprised. This thought surprises me" (*FBB* 61). Namjoshi's Miranda evolves through the narrative and she even reflects on the implications of the imperial privileges extended to her:

> He said I was a lady
> – it was my birthright –
> fit for a king.
> From his superior knowledge
> He made me dream.
> I listened
> and understood clearly
> in myself I was nothing.
>
> (*FBB* 64)

Once both Caliban and Miranda have seen through the patriarchal/imperial bias of Prospero's logic, they strike a bond between themselves, and find a place to dwell outside the definitions imperialist discourse has assigned them. Prospero is reduced to a mere old doodling fool, once the two repressed figures Caliban and Miranda find a way of coexisting without destroying each other. The poem thus underscores the need for female bonding and companionship to end the oppressive hegemony of patriarchy, and its most important tool of oppression – heterosexuality.

Namjoshi's re-telling of fables, myths and canonical stories successfully forces the reader to rethink the traditional patriarchal knowledge passed on from one generation to another through a variety of narratorial forms. Here is an attempt to revise the fragmented and distorted plots inherited from the past, and endow them with new meanings conceived from a female perspective. In doing this the writer creates her own version of new myths about women, rooted in female knowledge of female experience. These myths and stories perhaps are no more "true" than the old patriarchal literature. But they serve feminist purposes better. Moreover feminists are not particularly enamoured of absolute truths any way. What is more important is: "Where the old mythology was debilitating, the new is inspring" (Zimmerman 1990: 26).

Work Cited

de Beauvoir, Simone. *The Second Sex*. New York: Knoff, 1968.

Eliade, Mircia. *Myth and Reality*. New York: Harper & Row, 1963.

Jackson, Rosemary. *Fantasy: The Literature of Subversion*. London and New York: Methuen, 1981.

Koertge, Noretta. *Valley of the Amazons*. New York: St. Martin's Press, 1984.

Lamming, George. *The Pleasures of Exile*. London: Allison & Busby, 1984.

Namjoshi, Suniti. *Feminist Fables*. London: Sheba Feminist Publishers, 1981.

—. *From the Bedside Book of Nightmares*. Canada: Fiddlehead, 1984.

Radicalesbbians. "The Woman-Identified Woman." *Radical Feminisms*. Ed. Anne Koedt, Ellen Levine and Anita Rapone. New York: Quadrangle Books, 1973.

Rich, Adrienne. "When We Dead Awaken: Writing as Revision." *Adrienne Rich's Poetry*. Ed. Barbara Charles worth Gelpi and Albert Gelpi. New York: W.W. Norton & Company 1975: 90-99.

— *Of Woman Born: Motherhood as Experience and Institution*. New York: W.W. Norton, 1976.

Simon, Sherry. Review of *Feminist Fables*. *The Literary Criterion*. 1.20 (1985): 264-267.

Zimmerman, Bonnie. *The Safe Sea of Woman: Lesbian Fiction 1969-1989*. Boston: Beacon Press, 1990.

Zipes, Jack. *Don't Bet on the Prince: Contemporary Feminist Fairy Tales in North America and England*. Aldershot: Gower, 1986.

5

Feminist Fabulation: *The Conversations of Cow* and *The Mothers of Maya Diip*

In the last quarter of the twentieth century, feminist writing has appropriated a variety of literary forms and deployed them effectively for conveying feminist thought and ideology. Feminist writers erased patriarchal literary canons and mapped out new literary territories marked by woman-centered tales told from woman's perspective. These alternative narratives which function as a counter discourse and offer correctives to "patriarchy's problematic depictions of humanity," are often described as "feminist fabulations" (Barr 1992: XII). Feminist fabulation, above everything else, aims at exposing, subverting and rewriting the patriarchal myth of male superiority. It suggests the possibilities of living according to alternative myths and fictions and enables readers to pioneer spaces beyond patriarchal boundaries. The frequent use of fantasy---including the utopia and the dystopia---in the contemporary novel written by women constitutes both a response to the perceived absurdity of contemporary patriarchy and an impulse to envision an alternate reality that either corrects or exaggerates and exposes the ills of the present.

Some of the important features of feminist fabulation are: (i) creating new spaces which are outside the control of man-made laws and constructing alternative worlds which act as explicit/implicit comment on contemporary society and its discriminatory practices; (ii) developing fantasy narratives which expose the contradictions concealed by the conventions of realistic representation; (iii) projecting feminist vision of future in utopian/dystopian tales that deconstruct existing socio-cultural systems and expose the arbitrariness of all such constructs. (These texts encourage readers to contemplate a paradigm shift regarding human relations); (iv) employing metafictional devices which not only reveal the fictionality of fiction but also hint at the fictionality of the so called 'real', unmasking the constructed nature of patriarchal reality; (v) creating in fiction a space for free-floating signifiers thus releasing words from the fixity of meanings and (vi) urging the need for a cognitive transformation and rethinking of thinking itself.

'Feminist fabulation' is used here not as a generic term but as a descriptive label to signify feminist fiction "that offers us a world clearly and radically discontinuous from the patriarchal one we know, yet returns to confront that known patriarchal world in some feminist cognitive way" (Barr 1992: 10). This definition obviously owes its insight to Robert Scholes's conception of fabulation as "fiction that offers us a world clearly and radically different from the one we know, yet returns to confront that known world in some cognitive way" (1976: 47). Providing cognitive estrangement from the patriarchal world, therefore, is the primary function of feminist fabulation. This is done by projecting feminist visions which confront the patriarchal world. Conventionally, woman has been forced to live within patriarchal laws which relegate her to a secondary role and offer her no purpose beyond serving man. Feminist fabulation systematically demolishes these conventions and attempts to create a new future for women.

Fantasy is the single dominant aspect of feminist fabulation. If realistic literature and realism constitute the mainstay of the so called main (male?) stream literatures, feminists tend to break loose of the conventions of realistic mode of expression. Instead, they choose non-realistic forms because they hold that fantasy can explore areas of life that realist literature tends to deny or repress, concepts and ideas which fall outside the ideological compass of the contemporary real (Le Guin 1979: 43-45). Fantasy is what the real is not and so fantasy text necessarily traces the limits of the real. As a result, contradictions surface and the so called real is exposed as a construct which is arbitrary and ideologically determined.

Feminist writers, therefore, make fantasy their springboard in launching an attack on patriarchal 'reality'. Fantasy is a potentially subversive literary form and it enables the feminist writer to subvert not only other texts and literary forms but also the very means by which these texts and forms construe and construct the real. In a patriarchal society the experience of women is commonly ignored, invalidated and is denied a voice. Feminist fantasy explores the problems of *being* for women in a society which denies them subjectivity. It exposes the categories of the patriarchal real as arbitrary and maneuverable constructs and shows that the subordination of women is not a natural but an ideological process. Feminist fantasy takes different forms in women's fictional texts. One of the most popular of these is fabulating a fantasy world, "another world" which is different from and a critique of the contemporary society.

Namjoshi's *The Conversations of Cow* and *The Mothers of Maya Diip* may be best understood when read as works of feminist fabulation. In both these texts the author disrupts the language and genre by opening new spaces which privilege the lesbian as the place of alterity. The alternative world Namjoshi creates is that of women in love with women, and this brings to light the complicit connections between patriarchy and heterosexuality. In *Conversations* and *Mothers* Namjoshi engages in an interrogative dialogue with popular ideas about lesbianism such as considering lesbians as "other than women" and excluding them from motherhood. Historically sexologists and psychoanalysts define lesbian as a woman with masculine desires, 'a man trapped in a woman's body.' Again, lesbianism and motherhood have been considered mutually contradictory terms. Namjoshi interrogates these popular misnomers about lesbianism in *Conversations* and *Mothers*.

The Conversations of Cow does not belong to any known genre; it is a novella, a feminist utopian tale, a piece of speculative fiction, a lesbian *bildungsroman*, all in one. This erasure of boundaries between literary genres is important in the feminist enterprise of negotiating in-between spaces and creating new spaces. Namjoshi employs postmodernist techniques such as self-referentiality, unconventional plot structure and rupturing of all forms of realistic representation to tell the story of a lesbian coming to terms with her own identity. She does not use the autobiographical 'I' narrative; instead she inscribes herself, 'Suniti', as the central character in the novel. This allows her to look at her own experience from an outsider's perspective.

The Conversations of Cow is about a woman who is just coming to terms with being lesbian and is anxious to view her own identity as lesbian in the larger context of a heterosexual society. Suniti, the protagonist here, occupies a position of multiple marginalities. As a woman, a lesbian, a non-white immigrant in Canada she has no fixed identity. Gender, sexual preferences, race and nationality -- all these become free floating signifiers as Suniti constantly moves from one context to another. The education of Suniti lies in her coming to realize that the 'identity markers' are after all arbitrary constructs imposed by society, and that one can be what one chooses to be. The anxiety about self-definitions is lightened as the very notion of identity is played with in the course of the narrative.

Namjoshi presents the tale of Suniti as a fantasy fable. The novel begins with Suniti invoking the Cow of Thousand Wishes (*Kamadhenu* in the Hindu mythology) and setting out on a journey with the cow as her travelling companion. Suniti and the cow (by name Bhadravati or Baddy for short) both being lesbians strike a bond of kinship at once. Besides both are immigrants in Canada. Suniti, with her companion, visits the self-sustaining community of lesbian cows which stands for a kind of lesbian community. To find a lesbian companion and lesbian community constitute important phases in a lesbian's quest for self-awareness. "The lesbian community functions as an alternative society to heterosexual society providing the individual quest hero with validation, pride, joy and self-affirmation" (Zimmerman 1990: 120).

Once Suniti and Baddy form a lesbian companionship, then comes the logical question of "what next?" Suniti therefore asks the cow "... oughtn't there to be a logical pattern? Now that we are lovers, ought we not to get married for example?" (*CC* 89). In a heterosexual relationship lovers get married, start family, have children and live together. But in a lesbian relationship what possibly is the course of life open to lovers? More importantly, how will a lesbian couple find a place for themselves in the outside world governed by the laws of patriarchy? As Cowslip, one of the members of the community of lesbian cows, explains:

> The world .... is neatly divided into class A humans and class B humans. The rest don't count. How they look, walk and talk depends on television, but there are some factors which remain constant for several years. For example, Class A people don't wear lipstick, Class B people do. Class A people spread

> themselves out. Class B people apologise for so much as occupying space... Class A people never smile Class B people smile placatingly twice in a minute and seldom require any provocation.
>
> (*CC* 24)

If Baddy and Suniti are to find social approval, one of them must assume Class A role, and the other that of Class B.

Suniti's companion cow which can transform its form magically is willing to let Suniti take either role that pleases her. The cow may remain Bhadravati, if Suniti wants to take the male role. Alternatively, the cow can also turn into a white male 'Bud', and Suniti could become 'Sue' his beloved. Neither of these arrangements is satisfying to Suniti. She does not want to be a Grade B human, a mere appendage to male existence. In fact Suniti is a misogynist in the sense that she hates women who live and love according to patriarchal norms She resents patriarchy and she does not want to play the role of a man. In sum, she neither wants to be, or be with a man. Suniti expresses a bristling contempt for sexual role-playing.

Though a student of literature reared on patriarchal myth of male-centered universe, Suniti, now begins to see through these myths and understand the motives that inspired them. In fact, she has her own myth of the origin of mankind. She concludes that "men are aliens, unearthly aliens who descended from the Mars" (*CC* 90). She holds that men are invaders who come to earth after the space ships break down. These invaders gain control over planet earth "by means of mutation and biological manipulation and a massive mythologisation of the planetary purpose" (*CC* 92),

> ... man himself is right at the centre of the literary universe. Pigs and poodles, bats and babies, women and children, the earth itself, are always "the other". Now how to explain this inexplicable division, this perverse passion to make "the other" conform to the requirements of man's desire? It doesn't make sense, unless, of course, one starts with the postulate that men, in

fact are really Martians. Then all the pieces fit together.

(*CC* 92)

Suniti, therefore, prefers to stay away from these unlawful invaders thus opting to live in a separate, all-women community. Here Namjoshi is articulating a preference for a separatist feminist utopia.

After all this, what kind of relationship can a lesbian woman and a lesbian cow form?

Even though Suniti is free to choose the identity she wishes to possess, she finds it hard to make a choice. She does not want to be a man; nor a woman; she considers being a cow. But she realizes that *cow* is too broad a category and she may have to define her position in terms of sexuality, pedigree and so on. She considers being a snail since it is a bisexual creature. She feels like a poodle, a sheep, a gold fish by turns. She then chooses to be the lover. Soon she realizes that she cannot be like the conventional lover, since all declarations of love sound inane to her. She does not want to be the damsel in distress since she hates gallants. All possibilities she can consider are those she has acquired from language and literature, and these are again structures of patriarchy. How does she break away from these notions and basic structures of thought and feeling? The Cow acts as Suniti's guide in her quest for identity. She tells Suniti the story of Spindly Cow to drive home the point that one becomes what one thinks.

In her quest for identity Suniti considers various possibilities along a culturally constructed spectrum between masculinity at one end and femininity at the other. Within the dominant culture, masculinity and femininity are defined in a binary opposition to each another, and therefore a move away from one is simultaneously a move towards the other. Suniti refuses to be torn between the binaries, and looks for a free and neutral zone where the tyranny of gender does not operate. She also rejects the lesbian duplication of heterosexual categories such as butch and femme and searches for a position of alterity outside or beyond exclusive categories of woman and man. This quest is informed by the realization that all socially recognizable categories of gender are arbitrary and have no fixed significance. Namjoshi clearly indicates that a lesbian should not deploy dominant cultural terms of masculinity and femininity as a framework to comprehend a woman's desire for another woman. She parodies and subverts the conventional gender roles and rejects the masculine/feminine binarism.

The interchangeability of roles within lesbian sexuality subverts and exceeds the binarism of heterosexual masculinity and femininity which is fixed firmly according to gender. The fluidity of identity in the Suniti -- Cow relationship effects a series of reversals that disrupt the fixity and taken-for-grantedness of the conventional gender stereotypes in a heterosexual relationship. Central to Namjoshi's argument is the feminist concept of the distinction between biological sex and culturally constructed gender. The shared relationship of Suniti and the cow, and stories about their unusual experiences communicate the breakdown of fixed meanings in regard to gender, class or social roles. Transformation is the keyword here. The magic cow undergoes several transformations in order to facilitate the psychic transformation of Suniti.

In the last and final phase, Suniti encounters her own self as S2 and this section records Suniti's discovery that her true self should integrate her lesbianism with the rest of her personality. In the end, Suniti and S2 conjure up the Cow through incantation and invocation. The Cow reappears, and Suniti sets out to write *The Conversations of Cow*. The novel, in the typical metafictional manner, ends as Suniti begins to write down the story of her quest. In *The Conversations of Cow* the lesbian quester progresses from her initial tentativeness about her own lesbian identity to an assertion as well as celebration of the fact of being a lesbian. This evolution is made possible through the realization that all gender specific roles are restrictive and that liberation lies in breaking out of these moulds.

Namjoshi's novel parodies conventional quest narrative, although it is itself a novel of quest. The novelist makes use of the conventions of a quest narrative such as journey, meeting a mentor, inward journey or introspection and evolution of the protagonist through experience. These conventions provide a frame of reference for readers, orienting and directing their expectations. But the progression of the narrative belies these expectations and the readers are delighted and amused as they discover parodic manipulation of these conventions by the author. From 'quest' action to quest allegory is the movement here.

Even as Namjoshi was profoundly influenced by feminist thought and ideology, and wrote in the climate of 'identity politics', her work defies that context and her novels work to dismantle the humanist paradigm of singular and definitive identity. Instead, she plays with the notion of identity and rejects all notions of a unitary identity. It is useful to recall Sally Robinson's argument that identity be viewed as a process rather than a product in this context. To quote Robinson: "The idea that identity is a product rather than a process has as its corollary the humanist idea that gender and race are essences" (1991: 136). Once this structure is endorsed, the gendered and racial subjects – women and non-whites – are placed in singular positions in relation to hegemonic identities. Namjoshi cleverly topples all such essentialisms by looking at identity as something fluid, changing and evolving. In such a scheme of things, not only are all binaries – male vs female, white vs non-white, master vs slave etc. – deconstructed, but the very chain of being in which humans occupy a superior position over other species is demolished.

Namjoshi chooses to use non-realistic modes of narrative as she is dismissive of all traditional notions of reality. Furthermore, she seems to a have increasingly preferred the fantastic as an appropriate mode for feminist fabulation. The fictional world of *The Conversations* is a world of fantasy where women and cows live together and establish a lesbian continuum. The celestial cow can assume any form she chooses to: the cow appears and disappears, becomes a beautiful maiden and a handsome white man alternatively, shops, drives and loves like humans and is capable of magic charm. Fact and fiction, dream and reality, magic, metaphor and myth all mingle with each other providing a properly fluid atmosphere for the protagonist's experience of perpetually shifting identifies.

* * *

Alongside the contemporary stereotype of lesbian as 'other than woman' throughout the early part of this century, has run another equally pervasive stereotype of lesbian as 'being sterile'. Lesbian mother was almost considered a contradiction in terms. As Jackie Forster and Gillian Hanscombe point out in their study, the fallacious notion that lesbians are 'mannish' as well as 'manhaters', combined with people's failure to distinguish female sexual pleasure from the process of reproductive sex, has promoted the erroneous view that lesbians are incapable of conceiving and bearing children (1981: 1-38). So strongly entrenched were these notions that lesbians themselves sometimes internalized and endorsed them. Motherhood, therefore, very definitely becomes an issue for lesbian writers.

Adrienne Rich pointing out the importance of motherhood in the domain of sexual politics observes: "... motherhood is not only a core human relationship but political institution, a key stone to the domination in every sphere of women by men" (1980: 216). The contradictions of power/vulnerability which childbearing and childrearing involves for women has been a dominant motif in women's writing. The dichotomy of maternal power/female powerlessness in heterosexual societies comes in for a serious indictment in feminist/lesbian writing. "The patriarchal social order", it is argued, "responds to the threat which maternal power represents by imposing strict control on women's activities and restricting their access to the public sphere" (Palmer 1989: 100). Patriarchy's constructions of motherhood are called into question in feminist writing. This issue acquires additional urgency in the writing of radical lesbian feminists.

Women writers have explored the implications of motherhood and mothering in critical detail. A number of novels written in the 70's foreground the oppressive aspects of motherhood and depict how reproductive capacities render women vulnerable to male control, and consider childbirth and rearing painful and burdensome. Novels written in the 80's, in contrast, celebrate motherhood as a source of pleasure and power. Namjoshi's *The Mothers of Mayadiip* presents these contradictory viewpoints and attempts a critical analysis of their practical implications.

The novel begins with Jyanvi and her companion the Blue Donkey setting out for Maya Diip on the invitation of the Ranisaheb of this ancient matriarchy, off the west coast of India. Maya Diip is portrayed as a mythic island of all women, ruled by a benevolent matriarch in the manner of the ancient Rajahs of India. Maternity is the highest single ideal of this world, and all women here are mothers. Some are Grade A mothers or official mothers, some Grade B or biological mothers and some Grade 'C' or caretakers of children. The hierarchy of mothers is directly linked to the power structures in the kingdom. The matriarch is the supreme mother, and there are lesser matriarchs and chiefs of various guilds to assist her. A complex system of class operates in the Mayan island. The Matriarch and five great families monopolize power in reality, although they make the system appear perfectly democratic.

The question of succession is a sensitive one here. As Valerie, the European expatriate in Mayan island, explains: "In theory all the Daughters of Maya look to the Matriarch as an incarnation of the Supreme Mother; but in practice the blood line has been unbroken for seven hundred years" (*MM* 127). The kinship network is so designed that all loyalties flow in the direction of the Matriarch. The systems of power here operate much in the same way as they do in the world outside. The Matriarch is ably assisted by various guilds, prominent among them being the Guild of Therapists, the Guild of Poets and the Guild of the Servants of Goddess. The Poet's Guild repeats the dominant ideology in poetic language – playing the role of media in modern power systems. The Guild of the Servants of Goddess acts as the voice of religion. The Therapists' Guild is the Mayan equivalent of the police and they deal with all crimes of passion including non-conformity with Mayan customs. In fact any breach of Mayan conventions is seriously viewed by the Therapists' Guild.

Maya Diip is a lesbian island cut off from the heterosexual world outside, and its inhabitants are unaware of the systems of patriarchy. Reproduction here is totally controlled by the state. The pretty boys are milked for semen after which "they" dive into the sea and "turn into foam" (52). The semen thus collected is rationed out to women who qualify for motherhood. The mothers of Maya do not regard boys as children, but consider them "just as necessities" (*MM* 52-53). "Boys aren't the norm on Maya Diip. The boys fight among themselves. The mothers of Maya let them. Eventually there's nothing left to fight, only the waves. So they fight the waves, turn into foam, so to speak ...." (*MM* 160-161). As Asha the eldest daughter of the Matriarch opposes this cruelty against boys, she is branded an apostate and exiled from the kingdom.

In Maya Diip maternity is glorified and childrearing is considered the most sacred duty of mothers. They believe that "It's the duty of every Mayan to sacrifice herself for the welfare of children" (*MM* 146). A well-structured myth about the magnificence of motherhood is in circulation in the island. While Grade A mothers have proprietary rights over daughters, Grade C mothers simply do the chores for children. It is through hardwork and perseverance that a Grade C mother can hope to move up the hierarchy. Jyanvi is appalled by the subtle class distinction that privileges some Mayans over the rest, and begins to question the hypocrisy of the whole system of mothering and childrearing.

The successor to the throne is chosen by the Oracle, and the Oracle can be manipulated by the Matriarch. When the Matriarch declares Saraswati as the choice of the Oracle, the other two daughters, Shyamila the civil and Pramila the poet, conspire along with Sarla Devi the chief of the Guild of the Servants of Goddess, and effect a deft coup deposing the Matriarch from power and sending her off into the forest. Along with the Matriarch Saraswati, Jyanvi and the Blue donkey too are banished from the Mayan kingdom.

In the forest the exiles encounter another social system – Ashagad. The banished daughter of the Matriarch, Asha is the founder of this society and she reigns supreme over a kingdom of all men. Ashans have their own myth and legend. Ashagad is a direct inversion/mirror image of the island of Maya. Motherhood is important here too, and boys qualify to motherhood after passing tests and attaining adult status. They cannot hope to be biological mothers; they pray to the Tree of Life under which they find babies. These obviously are the pretty boys abandoned by the Mayans. Asha the Empress has founded the Ashan kingdom broadly on the ideals she imbibed as a Mayan: the glorification of motherhood is the principal among them. When Valerie mentions the patriarchal system where Mayans and Ashans live together and the latter dominate and enslave the former, the inhabitants of Ashagad are appalled. The possibility of Ashans enslaving Mayans and forcing them to have their babies, however outrageous, sets the Ashan boys thinking. The concept of having their own branded children appeals to them. The Empress Asha holds Valerie responsible for corrupting innocent Ashans and puts her in solitary confinement.

In the next movement, male androids descend in Ashagad in search of new recruits to their army. They are equipped with a sophisticated system of communications and possess the most powerful arms. In fact, they get a message about Valerie's imprisonment on their SOS beam and come to rescue her. However, Valerie prefers solitary confinement in Ashagad to returning to the fold of the androids.

The androids are primarily traders – technical advancement and sophistication is their particular strength. They follow a military regime and by and large uphold the values of a male dominated society. They are not, however, real men but androids built to a specific stereotype. They are so conditioned to perfection that the real men are expected to approximate to the models set by them. As Androids are primarily traders they insist Ashagad enters into a trade agreement with them. Ashagad has nothing to sell and Ashans don't see the usefulness of the shiny dollars that Androids offer. When all talks of trade fail, they blame the Ashan leader for her autocratic ways and depose her "for obstructing the causes of democracy and justice" (*MM* 103). They appoint "a new government that'll be more cooperative and loyal" to them (*MM* 103). They take the Matriarch, Asha, Saraswati, Jyanvi and the Blue donkey as hostages and leave Ashagad temporarily in the custody of Madhu and other Ashan boys with the hope that the young men would appreciate "that it wasn't okay to be ruled by women." (*MM* 104) The high-handed behaviour of these mechanized male androids sounds quite familiar since it is clearly reminiscent of the autocracy of the so called advanced nations in contemporary world.

These androids are in reality an 'abandoned experiment' – the helicopter in whose belly they were abandoned turned into a protective mother, fed them, shaped them and turned them into men, not ordinary men but TV heroes. As real life models were not available to them, they emulated TV heroes they could see on the videotapes available to them on board. They plan to sell their female hostages to the land of Paradise, but in the meanwhile the helicopter shudders and heads for an emergency landing. Jyanvi and other hostages inflate their life jackets, dive downwards and land in Paradise.

The social structure of Paradise is totally different from that of Maya Diip or Ashagad. Society here is divided into two categories: Mothers and Gallants. Mothers are fewer in number, and they are regarded as the embodiment of romantic ideals of beauty, freedom, love and happiness. Gallants are far more numerous and their prime concern is to win the favour of mothers. Therefore, they woo mothers in song and verse with acts of worship and gallantry. Since there is an acute shortage of mothers in Paradise, many gallants are often left with no object to direct their worship to. Quite a few of them commit suicide in despair. The roles are clearly differentiated and "two of a kind may not pair" (*MM* 232). So gallants cannot make friends with gallants they have to live and die as suitors and supplicants of mothers.

Paradise is believed to have been founded by a Mayan princess who sailed away in search of beauty. An extreme idealism is fundamental to Paradise. Since the founder of the kingdom was a princess, they use feminine gender for everyone. Gender is of no consequence here; the only distinction noticed is the one between Mothers and Gallants.

The gallants of Paradise are overjoyed to find mothers of Maya in their island and they immediately set out to woo them. The matriarch of Maya Diip and the queen of Paradise arrive at an understanding: Paradise has an acute shortage of mothers; the Matriarch of Maya needs the help of gallants to regain her authority in Maya Diip. It would, therefore, be appropriate to use the services of gallants to restore Maya Diip to the lawful Matriarch, and in return the gallants could have some of the mothers of Maya Diip. Elaborate arrangements for war ensue, and when the Matriarch returns to Maya Diip with her impressive entourage, she is of course more than welcome.

Once lawful order is restored, the Matriarch decides to retire into the forest with the Blue donkey for her companion.

In a quick and unexpected turn of events, Jyanvi is made the successor to the throne of Maya Diip. Ironically, Jyanvi who is the only 'non-mother' becomes the Matriarch of Maya Diip at last. It is an act of subversion, and undermines the popular discourses that glorify mother and motherhood. The individual and independent identity of woman is asserted.

The Mothers of Maya Diip has all the features of a feminist dys(u)topia: defamiliarization achieved through strange characters and incidents, creation of an imaginary world very different from the real, journey, quest and so on. Namjoshi presents not a single utopian world but multiple worlds each following its own pattern of social organization. There are as many as four models of human society: Maya Diip an all-woman state, Ashagad an all-men world headed by a matriarch, the world of male androids and the Paradise full of gallants constantly engaged in wooing mothers. Whatever may be the permutation and combination of male-female relationships, the old repressive structures of heterosexual relationships return in explicit or disguised form in all these systems. As the naïve visitor, who is a witness to the goings on in all the places, Jyanvi serves to focus our responses. The Blue donkey plays the role of a guide in a traditional utopia. The interaction between the utopian society and the visitor from the present reveal that both worlds are culturally bound and therefore subject to change.

Maya Diip despite being a lesbian community and matriarchy is far from being perfect. Here women are regarded not as individuals but as mothers. Besides the misoandric practice of Mayans, their internal squabbles and power struggles prevent the readers, from perceiving Maya Diip as perfect or permanent. Each of these societies – Maya Diip, Ashagad, Paradise is conjured up as an alternative and is exposed as flawed. A tone of playfulness is central to the narrative, and the author invites the readers to see the text as a game and to participate in the creative process. In other words, the reader is encouraged not to dedicate herself to some absolute utopian vision but rather to make and unmake multiple worlds, and learn to experiment with alternative realities.

It is interesting to note that the protagonists in both these novels – Suniti and Jyanvi -- are artists, writers. One of the basic forms of the developmental novel is the *Kunstlerroman* or portrait of the artist, which connects the creation of the self to the creation of a work of art. In *The Conversations of Cow* Suniti's journey toward self-understanding and self-acceptance ends as she sits down to write the story of conversations. Writing of a book, in this case is both the means and metaphor for the creation of the lesbian self. Furthermore, since the evolution of a lesbian is largely shrouded in silence in contemporary societies, it is quite natural that the lesbian hero is often a writer or an artist. Jyanvi in *The Mothers of Maya Diip* is a poet: she initially falls out of favour with the Matriarch of Maya Diip for reciting the song of a non-mother; but eventually becomes the personal poet of the Matriarch as the latter appreciates the truth of her poetry. Jyanvi also composes an epic poem to inspire the gallants in their war on Maya Diip and she is ultimately raised to the position of the Matriarch of Maya Diip. To be articulate is important for a lesbian writer, and this need is reflected in their choice of a poet/writer for their protagonist.

The fantasy tales offer the feminist writer a number of conventions which can be used to construct a story in which the writer can de-naturalize institutions as well as institutionalized modes of behaviour, the reality of contemporary world as well as realist forms of representation. Reading feminist fantasy stories can be a new way of seeing and understanding the nature and operation of contemporary society. As readers learn 'to listen to dragons', to use Le Guin's expression, they will be freed from the tyranny of the 'real'.

Works Cited

Barr, S. Marleen. *Feminist Fabulation: Space/Postmodern Fiction*. Iowa City: University of Iowa Press, 1992.

Forster, Jackie, and Hanscombe Gillian. *Rocking the Cradle -- Lesbian Mothers: a challenge in family living*. London: Peter Owen, 1981.

LeGuin, Ursula K. *The Language of the Night: Essays on Fantasy and Science Fiction*. Ed. Susan Wood. New York: G.P. Putnam, 1979.

Namjoshi, Suniti. *The Conversations of Cow*. London: The Womens Press, 1985.

---. *The Mothers of Maya Diip*. London: The Womens Press, 1989.

Palmer, Paulina. *Contemporary women's fiction: Narrative practice and feminist theory*. Jackson & London: University Press of Mississippi, 1989.

Robinson, Sally. *Engendering the Subject: Gender and Self-representation in Contemporary Women's Fiction*. Albany: State University of New York Press.

Rich, Adrienne. *Of Lies, Secrets and Silence: Selected Prose 1966-1978*. London: Virago, 1980.

Scholes, Robert. "The Roots of Science Fiction". *Science Fiction: A Collection of Essays*. Ed. Mark Rose. Englewood Cliffs: Prentice Hall, 1976. 46-56.

Zimmerman, Bonnie. *The Safe Sea of Women: Lesbian Fiction 1969-1989*. Boston: Beacon Press, 1990.

6

Writing as Play: *The Blue Donkey Fables* and *Saint Suniti and the Dragon*

After the overtly political re-reading of canonical texts and violent rejection of patriarchal norms in *The Bedside Book of Nightmares*, Namjoshi turned to a more light-hearted play with ideas, ideologies and identities in her next set of fables called *The Blue Donkey Fables*. These were written in 1986-87 at the request of the Women's Press, and as Namjoshi herself acknowledges, inspiration for these comic, satiric sketches on contemporary life came from Jonathan Swift and Lewis Carroll – the two master storytellers of the fantastic. It is the exuberance of Swift's imagination and the inventiveness of his imaginary that appeals to Namjoshi most. She is also fascinated by "the breathtakingly rapid satirical play" in Swift's work (1989: 103). From Lewis Carroll she has learnt how one can effect paradigm shifts, playing with structures and systems. Combining these two skills – imaginative inventiveness and logical comprehension of systems, she creates fascinating tales/verses about a range of issues from creation to subsurfacesonics, poetic practice to endangered Pandas. Namjoshi is not in any anxiety to make a political or feminist point here; she simply engages in a play with traditional texts, contemporary social norms, gender stereotypes, classical myths, and all notions of order and reality. Furthermore, Namjoshi plays with poetic practice, linguistic codes and formal conventions. In doing so, she rejects all kinds of essentialism and dispenses with the old dualities.

In Western feminist critical theory there has been a resistance to viewing women's writing as play because playfulness is generally associated with a lack of purpose or seriousness. As Arendt explains: "All serious activities, irrespective of their fruits, are called labor, and every activity which is not necessary either for the life of the individual or for the life process of society is subsumed under playfulness ....." (1958: 127-128). Theorists, therefore, are wary of likening women's writing to play since such an interpretation might diffuse the revolutionary potential of this body of writing. Play has been traditionally associated with children and looked upon as a child's imitation of the adult ways of living (Freud 1961: 10-11). By an extension of the same logic, considering women's writing as play might equate it with women's effort at imitating male ways of living, and implicate women in patriarchy.

A close study of women's texts, however, clearly reveals women writers' playful preoccupation with the dominant discourse. This playfulness is a sign of maturity and not of naivete. Patriarchy no longer can create insecurity in them since they have learnt to play about with the myths and mores of patriarchy. This signifies that women writers have begun to experience the joy of release and make light of the oppression of the dominant discourse and culture. As Patricia Yaegar rightly points out: "When we take the weight of patriarchy – its force and inevitability – too seriously, we miss a great deal of what goes on in women's texts" (1988: 227). It is, therefore, important that we do not miss the delight offered by the de-constructive energy of women's texts.

To this discussion one may as well add an insight from Indian aesthetics to. 'Play' in the Indian context has a connotation of creativity implied in it. In fact every act is viewed upon as 'play' and such a metaphysic would create slippages, between dream and reality and move reality itself in new directions. Above everything else, the pleasures of play and joys of creation may be viewed as akin to each other. The fact that Namjoshi's work being discussed in this chapter reflects the writer's playful mood and intent to delight has warranted such a detailed discussion of the poetics of play with respect to women's writing. I have established a theoretical matrix in which it is possible to conceive of play as a way of making light what is repressive and as a refusal to be oppressed by the dominant systems.

The Blue Donkey Fables comprises more than seventy short pieces -- some in prose, some in verse -- all marked by an unmistakable sense of mirth. There is criticism -- criticism of the anamolies of contemporary world -- but it evokes mirth and laughter more than rage or revenge. The fictional world of these tales is peopled by talking beasts and birds, and incidents included are absurd and incongruous such as one-eyed monkey going into print, parrots and tortoise planning the creation of a planet sans human beings, a cat engaging in poetic practice, three piglets going in for an aptitude test and so on. The narrator views on this anomalous, incongruous, absurd world in a mood of detached amusement and uses an ironic tone in narration. It is important to notice, however, that the absurdities in the animal world described here are actually a mimicry of what goes on in the human world.

The Blue Donkey is the central character in a number of these tales. She is the sanest and the wisest of all, and often human beings who interact with her emerge as ridiculous figures. For instance, in the first story the councillors feel that a blue donkey sitting by the bright red bridge is anamolous and insist that she either change her colour into an inoffensive grey or move away. The donkey refuses to move and the councillors begin to debate the conduct of the donkey, but cannot come to an agreement about the alternative course of action. They "argued and squabbled and argued" until they almost get used to the blueness of the donkey (*BF* 2). Very few could see that blueness is innate to the donkey. Most councillors fail to see such an obvious point and hence become objects of ridicule.

The Blue Donkey acquires fame as a tourist attraction, and turns into a source of income for the town. When she grows old and turns grey, the townsfolk are worried. The Donkey offers to retire and turn into a legend. But when the people of the town spread a story that the Blue Donkey is no more, she protests against such blatant lying, goes public and declares that she is alive and has only changed her colour. This causes a great excitement and becomes a media event.

The Mayor and the townsfolk rejoice at the excitement caused by the controversy, and the Blue Donkey having done her duty retires again. But the Donkey has realized that there is no such thing as absolute truth since the listener chooses to hear what he/she wants to. The Blue Donkey, therefore, turns into a writer and her disciples write down the stories she narrates to them. The safest form of lying is creative writing!

The Blue Donkey narrates tales based on her own experiences to her disciples. Fables have always been used for didactic purpose since the days of Aesop. Blue Donkey, however, does not attempt explicit moralization. Instead, she provides her disciples with riddle-like tales to reflect upon. These tales cover a variety of subjects ranging from the predicament of a poet to conventional notions of heroism, and the ironic sting is usually in the tail piece of the tale. "Dusty Distance", for instance, tells about Blue Donkey's quest for fortune. She realizes that it is not easy to make a career as a poet and settles down for a part-time job for half a carrot! Some times a familiar moral emerges from an unfamiliar set of incidents. In "The Sinner" the Blue Donkey suggests that a sinner cannot ask for absolution unless he/she had done penance. The title character, a grey donkey, commits no sin except being disrespectful to the Blue Donkey, but is instructed to do the penance and seek redemption! The author trivializes the high-sounding ethical concepts such as sin, redemption, penance and punishment by textualising them in unfamiliar contexts.

The Blue Donkey also fabricates new fables for changing times and comes up with new morals that upset the conventional ethical norms. Survival is the highest ethic in a world of cut throat competition and mercenary exploitation. In "Vulgar Streak" the Blue Donkey's message is: crudeness can only be tackled crudely. Some trickery is necessary for self-preservation. "In Doubled and Redoubled" a magpie decides to prove that the Blue Donkey is no wise sage but a fraud. She, therefore, spreads the news that the Blue Donkey can accomplish miracles like turning straw into gold. This draws a hoard of beasts to the Blue Donkey. They insist that she perform the miracle and turn the straw into gold. The Blue Donkey decides to tackle trickery with cleverer trickery. So she tells them that she has transferred half of her gift to the magpie in return for the latter's faith. The magpie, therefore, can turn the straw into gold and the Blue Donkey turns the gold into straw again. The Blue Donkey points to the straw in front of them and adds that it demonstrates double miracle. The animals go away content, and the magpie stays behind fearing the displeasure of the Blue Donkey. The Blue Donkey is instead pleased and remarks: "Two miracles, in the course of a day, two saints where at first there were none – we did rather well" (*BF* 82). Blue Donkey fables thus provide instructions for a practical way of life and for an amicable coexistence.

There are some tales retold from classical myths in this

collection. Some of the familiar figures from classics such as Athene, Medusa, Circe, Scylla and Eurydice emerge altered. The alteration is effected by changing the point of view, and viewing the experiences of these women from a female perspective. The old stories are charged by "female knowledge of female experience so that they can no longer stand as foundations of collective male fantasy" (Ostriker 1985: 318). The altered figures function as correctives to the stereotypes and turn into retrieved images of what women have collectively and historically suffered: They are, in some cases "instructions for survival" (Ostriker 1985: 318).

Athene in Namjoshi's "Olive Branch" is unhappy that she is always identified as 'her father's daughter'. Having sprung from her father Jove's forehead she has no place in matriarchal linealogy. The questions of identity and gender are important for goddesses too. Athene is therefore anxious to acquire a new identity in the changing times. She tells her companion owl: "Don't you understand that the times have changed and that in accordance with the times I have to change my image?" (*BF* 46). The Owl quickly invents a female tradition for her mistress: earth is her mother, and the owl her sister. That's how Athene and the owl get incorporated into the world of women. "Scylla: An Exegesis" is a re-inscription of Virgil's man-eating monster. There is a certain propriety, Namjoshi argues, in Scylla's hatred. She is scorned and thrown into the sea by the man she loved and reemerges as a hateful monster devouring men. There is one point which still remains perplexing: "What did the men she swallowed want to be?" (*BF* 53). This interrogative closure opens up the story of Scylla for further speculation and exploration.

Namjoshi's Medusa is a quiet creature "who troubled no one", but lived in peaceful coexistence with fish and birds. Perseus, therefore, pleads with the Gorgon to look at him (*BF* 59). Eurydice of Namjoshi flees from Orpheus since she realizes that the latter after all "was not Death's master, but a slave" like her. The Homeric Earth Goddess and sorceress Circe who turns Odysseus's fellow sailors to beasts and who through out Western literature represents the evil magic of female sexuality appears to be a positively charming woman to the persona in "On that Island ...". The power of Circe to turn men into pretty piglets is much admired and asserted.

Namjoshi attempts a re-telling of some of the more recent parables too. For instance, the three monkeys in her tale "Ivory Apes" imitate their wise ancestors and turn into "No sisters". They could see, hear and speak no evil. They turn this position into a strategy and refuse to see, hear or speak good either. How are they to know what is good and what is bad, any way? Namjoshi reinvents old parables, re-imagines popular characters from classics, and urges a review of the conventional forms of cognition.

What Namjoshi does here is to repeat the stories from the past introducing clever subversions into the original stories, marginalizing the monumentality of canonical versions and mocking at their claim to authenticity. Consequently the discriminatory knowledge that the canonical discourses embody is de-constructed and the normative values upheld by the patriarchal culture are systematically demolished. The role-reversals, plot-inversions and subversions in Namjoshi's work produce humour that is at once pleasant, provocative and rebellious.

Much of the mirth of these tales springs from the subtle shifting of the point of view to beasts and birds. Namjoshi often makes her animals – blue donkey, tiger, one-eyed monkey, cat, toad, tortoise and so on – look on and judge the human world from their own perspective. Most things which appear important and significant may turn out to be ridiculous and inconsequential, the perspective thus altered. For instance, the little bird Robin advises the self-righteous saint thus: "Acquit/yourself of a superior wisdom, love/whom you can O you silly saint/There's nothing to it" (*BF* 16). The hierarchy humans impose on nature in order to privilege themselves is ridiculed by birds and beasts. In "Prodigal Pussy", the pet cat insists that she and her mistress love each other on equal terms. In "Creation: Plan B" tortoises and parrots draft a plan for the creation of a new world. They keep humans out of their scheme and so live happily ever after.

"Magpie" is a delightful short tale in which the contrasting attitudes of a bird and a woman to wealth are juxtaposed. A magpie finds a gold coin and is delighted by its glint and glitter. A woman tries to get it from the bird since the latter does not "understand the value of money" any way. But the Magpie refuses to part with the glittering piece of gold. The woman offers to give ten shining pieces in exchange of one piece of gold planning to cheat the bird by giving her bits of tinsel. The bird turns down the offer. The woman is exhausted at the folly of the bird and asks: "Didn't you understand everything I said?" The Magpie says "yes" and the woman demands: "What did you understand? The bird aptly sums up: "That money glitters. That ten is equal to one sometimes, and sometimes it isn't. And that justice, as you said, is strictly for the birds" (*BF* 55). The bird's arithmetic and logic are both impeccable!

Some of these stories not merely ridicule or laugh at the vanities of humans but launch a direct attack on man's interference in the world of beasts. "The Purposeless Pandas" is an ironic tale which articulates the response of pandas to the environmentalists' zeal to preserve an endangered species. The so called friends of beasts provide the pandas with cans of proteins and safely enclosed spaces to live in. For purposes of publicity they wish to take some photographs of pandas playing and mating. The good natured pandas gently protest and refuse to indulge in such activities in the mid-afternoon. When their enthusiastic friends leave them to themselves for the day, Pandas leave a note and vanish. The note reads thus: "We are no longer endangered. Please consider us as quite extinct" (*BF* 91).

Namjoshi often indulges in metatextual musings in this anthology. She does a lot of loud thinking about poetic practice, what it means to be a poet, the craft of poetry and other related issues. There are poems about poets and poems, readers and critics as well as the whole business of writing poetry. She parodies earlier poets by plagiarizing them, satirizes stereotypical similes and metaphors, has a dig at reviewers and critics, ridicules the calculative commercial publishers and exposes the goings on in the contemporary literary scenario. By treating the world of literary writing, publishing and reviewing with playfulness, Namjoshi reduces the so-called intellectual practices from the important place they generally occupy to a manageable absurdity. 'A Tale of Triumph', for instance, addresses the absurdity of contemporary criticism. The Blue Donkey here complains that a critic has denied her existence on the grounds that she is after all an imaginary beast. The Blue Donkey too could have ignored the existence of the critic but it is not "a homicidal beast" (*BF* 41). That makes the difference!

A number of tales in this anthology carry autobiographical undertones. Namjoshi articulates her own experiences of writing and publishing poetry in half serious, half comic narratives. In "Explanation", for instance, Namjoshi answers the question often asked of her as to why she chooses to write about plants and animals and not people:

> The cat charmed me.
> The tree disarmed me.
> And though the real people
> hadn't yet harmed me,
> I thought that they would
> given the chance.
>
> (*BF* 7)

In "One-eyed Monkey Goes into Print" Namjoshi satirizes the publishers' resistance to publish animal tales. When one-eyed Monkey tries to publish her book: "The Life and Learning of a One-eyed Monkey" the publishers turn it down on the grounds that "the title was lacking in human interest" (*BF* 8). After several foiled attempts, the book gets published under the title "The Amorous Adventures of a One-eyed Mynx" and achieves a moderate success. While the truthful monkey does not recognise herself in this new version, enthusiastic reviewers find autobiographical element in these tales. All conventions of reading, reviewing and publishing come in for a serious indictment here.

In "Poetic Practice", the clever cat prints her paw on a piece of paper and calls it 'concrete verse.' "Poem against Poets" is an obvious parody of romantic poetry and begins with the oft quoted lines of Shelly from "Ode to the West Wind": "I fall upon the thorns of life,/I weep, I bleed" (*BF* 22). Namjoshi suggests that poetry need not be always about nightingales, roses and the like, and poets should realise that "there are other/more ordinary animals." Then the poet ironically adds: "They are not literary/They own their pain" (*BF* 22). Again in "Stilted Poem", Namjoshi satirizes poetic conventions and asks: What, after all the usual confessions of love or compliments to the lover, does a poem articulate? It "stutters and stops. Then spills into life" (*BF* 89). "Craft" is about poets who turn their 'art' into craft, into a sort of industry and engage in profitable writing or 'fabricating the necessary lies' (*BF* 69). What does it mean to be a poet? Namjoshi has a practical, down to earth response to offer "... a poet lives/like any other creature, talks perhaps/more than is normal, her doom no brighter/nor her death less dismal than any other" (*BF* 98). There is a poem addressed to the readers too. This is an analysis of the process of transmission of a text. Namjoshi has always believed in a reader-friendly text and the active involvement of readers in the making of meaning. The author is no tyrant to define and control the entire sphere of meaning. "... it takes two live bodies, one/writing and one reading, to generate a sky,/a habitable planet and a working sun" (*BF* 51). The writer and the reader may or may not agree, yet the two need to engage in a dialogue to make a text meaningful.

There are stories about gender discrimination which point to the difficulties of being a woman in a male-dominated society. The inevitable/inviolable hierarchy that controls all relationships in the world is the theme of "Turf". A Frog occupies a small piece of turf and feels pleased with itself; the cat who lives as the mistresse's pet in the house lets the frog to its vain claims since frogs don't matter much; the cat in turn is pleased with its place in the house and the mistress leaves the cat to its whims since cats matter little. Finally the master divorces the mistress, the mistress and her pet are dislodged from the premises, while the frog remains safe in its corner. The familiar questions of power and proprietorship are raised and sited in a rather unfamiliar context here.

In "The Bride" the king is in search of a worthy wife for his highly accomplished son -- the prince, the future heir to the kingdom. He conducts a series of contests and shortlists winners in various contests for beauty, strength, knowledge, intelligence, wit and skills such as music and archery. They are presented to the prince and some of them have credentials better than those of the Prince. A slighty nervous prince mutters: "... they seem to be lacking in the womanly qualities" and the wordly-wise king clarifies: "I have weeded these out, you can now choose from those who did not compete" (*BF* 57). The most feminine of feminine virtues is to stay out of all competition.

Gods in "The Fortunate One" shower blessings on a little girl. They make her a queen, give her a good husband, five children, seventeen grandchildren, health, intelligence, beauty and long life with one proviso that she should be "responsible". At the end of her long life she faces gods feeling a little guilty that she couldn't retain any of the gifts given to her: beauty, health, money or power over words. Gods are not displeased; in fact they are happy that she has often failed. Otherwise she would cease to be human and turn into a god herself. That humans should err is a fact of life welcome to gods! Here is a variation of *felix culpa*!

"Ordinary Women" is an interestingly analytical subversion of conventional roles and role expectations. The categories such as knights, kings and ladies are all invested with certain role-specific traits. For instance, knights are expected to play the saviours and the ladies are always to be rescued. Knights are to woo the gentle ladies and the latter are meant to be wooed. Amidst these conventions how does one locate a woman in love with another woman? The persona here finds a way out of this predicament and tells the woman she woos "we love one another like two ordinary women." But her love is unwilling to give up her claims to ladyship. Then the persona solves the problem by suggesting, "You are a lady and I am a lesbian". The speaker subtly changes the terms of the equation by replacing the knight first with the ordinary woman, and then with the lesbian.

Changing of forms and identities by wearing masks and animal skins is a common occurrence in fables. Since fables are essentially meant to effect a transformation, transformation of physical forms becomes a natural component of the major overarching theme of change. What one should emphasize about Namjoshi's fables besides their obvious feminist reversals of meaning is the author's play with narrative representation and framing – investing animals with narratorial authority, inclusion of texts within texts in curious ways and a carnivalesque accumulation of intertexts ranging from the Bible to classical mythology, the lives of saints, fairy tales, fables and beast tales from various traditions. Use of humour to create instabilities and moments of self-directed irony is the hallmark of her style.

* * *

Suniti Namjoshi continues to play with ideas, ideologies, concepts and literary texts of the past in her next book, *Saint*

Suniti & The Dragon (1994). As the title suggests, this book is about Suniti's quest for sainthood and her encounters with the dragon. Like much of Namjoshi's earlier work, this too is allegorical in nature: the novel is not so much about canonization as about deviation from the path of virtue which is an essential aspect of the human condition. The author is considering here one of the most popular themes of literary and philosophic discourse -- the question of evil. In doing this she freely draws on a variety of mythical and literary sources. "Saint Suniti and the Dragon", the allegorical title, at once brings to our mind the patron saint of England, St. George, the adventurous hero who rode up on his white charger, overcame the dragon and delivered the princess. Besides there are direct albeit playful references to the national epic of Anglosaxons – *Beowulf*. Suniti's encounters with the dragon are counterpointed with Beowulf's battles with Grendel and his mother, the demonic creatures who harass virtuous people. One cannot miss the echoes of the *Book of Genesis* and the myth of the fall, the central myth of English literature. Namjoshi makes intertextual references to a number of earlier texts establishing curious parallels with the world of the past through parody, pastiche and playful allusion. There are, for instance, references to the jewelled serpent in the blissful garden, which invariably invoke not only the Biblical tale but also Milton's recreation of the same in *Paradise Lost*. Again, "Songs of Despair" are reminiscent of Blake's songs, but present a vision of good and evil that is contradictory to Blakean interpretation.

Suniti's (mis)adventures with the dragon are presented in twelve brief episodes in the manner of (mock) epic tales. In fact, the thematic motifs of quest and journey and the protagonist's evolution through her experiences with evil place *Saint Suniti and the Dragon* in the genre of quest novels and link it with Dante's *The Divine Comedy* the cult text of this genre. Like in Dante's work, the poetic journey to the life beyond is actually a representation of *this* world *here*. However it is important to note that Namjoshi's text in most cases holds an enigmatic relationship with the earlier literary texts it invokes. Most of these allusions are likely to produce complex reactions in the reader, for the author is linking two worlds and asking the reader to compare them. With a literary allusion, an entire work is activated and as the readers discover patterns of comparison and differences between the texts and the worlds contained in them, they experience the pleasure of playing a guessing game or sharing a kind of private joke with the writer.

The protagonist here is Suniti, obviously the author's alter ego, and the dragon symbolizes evil. Suniti's quest for sainthood and her encounter with evil operate on three levels: at the psychological level, one should come to terms with one's inner fears, monsters of ones own making; next at the quotidian level one needs to come to terms with the world around on a day-to-day basis; finally at the wider historical and political level there is a great deal of evil manifesting in the form of war and socio-political violence, and an individual feels totally helpless faced with such violence. Suniti's quest registers these three phases and in each phase she moves closer to an understanding of evil though no where near conquering it.

The quest begins with the protagonist's desperate attempt to find her goddess in "the round stone, all belly and no bone", "in the white bone, all elegance, finely honed", and "in all walking, waking women she had met" (*SS* 1). From all the innumerable flowers -- pansies, irises, roses and above all gilded lilies -- and the courage with which they die in the light of the Sun, Suniti apprehends a rather inimitable ideal -- facing extinction without fear. Traditionally, canonization requires among other things a definite proof that the person in question wrought miracles during her/his lifetime. The chances of attaining sainthood in modern life get slimmer because it is not easy to get people believe in miracles any longer. To become a saint, it is important to be recognized as one by people around. In "Failed Prayers", an angel plucks iridescence from the casual air and offers it to Suniti. Suniti's problem is "would any one else believe in it?" Failure to work miracles dampens Suniti's aspirations for sainthood.

In the next step, the protagonist tries to cast off pride and also inner fear. Suniti tells herself: "If I could face Death unafraid, then surely I would be a Conquering Maid?" (*SS* 5). Suniti sets out to locate fear, and this quest takes her not into "a forest among benign trees", but on to rock hard pavements "crowded with people". Paradoxically fear is frightened by people! Suniti finds fear safely ensconced within her, dissolved in her own blood. How can she kill fear which is spread into each of her capillaries? In a typical Namjoshi subversive move that follows, the relation between Suniti and the dragon is inverted and transformed. Dragon is generally portrayed prostrating at the feet of a saint: but here Suniti finds herself at the feet of the dragon "puzzled and puny" (*SS* 6). Altering the original images, breaking parallels which have been established, frustrating stereotypical expectations of readers – all these are a part of the writer's playful engagement with conventional texts and concepts, and the reader who has by now grasped the rules of the game becomes the coplayer perceiving new patterns of thought that emerge from the inversions and subversions of stereotypes.

"The Trials of the Saint" is a reworking of the many tales of martyrdom in general and of Beowulf in particular. Grendel's Mama, in Namjoshi's version, in her search for food for her hungry son finds Suniti the protagonist a suitable prey. Suniti tries to strike a sisterly bond with Grendel's ma, and promises to find a sumptuous meal for the hungry monster. Suniti, after a great deal of searching finds a herd of cows and suggests that Grendel could feed on them. Grendel, however, eats nothing other than human flesh. Suniti is helpless and almost gets reconciled to the fate of ending up as a meal to the monster, but the latter rejects her as he insists on being fed on the flesh of "a proper woman". As Grendel does not find her "a proper woman" Suniti is saved. The question, however, is how can she aspire for sainthood when she does not even qualify for proper womanhood?

Suniti almost gives up hopes of becoming a saint, but her friends advise her to look for a proper saint who could inspire her. Speculating on the possible locations of saints, they suggest that saints live in paradise, in solitude, in obscurity, and perhaps in India. Suniti continues her quest along these lines. In paradise where everything is plentiful, she almost feels like a saint; alone in a glass bottle adrift on the sea she gets the feeling of leading a blameless life; in a state of oblivion every one is a saint. In India there are not only saints but many saintlikes and it is not easy to distinguish one from the other.

In the next unit, "The Line Up", Namjoshi interrogates all conventional notions of sainthood. All saints are martyrs of sorts, and the capacity to suffer is considered a necessary qualification for sainthood. But beautiful saints with bloodied lips are, after all, artists' creations. The second candidate for canonization boasts of thirty years of struggle. Does a bludgeoned brain and battered body qualify one for sainthood? The third claims an inward gaze and she is indifferent to be seen or to see. With "Saint and Martyr" etched in acid on her brow, she evokes pity and no reverence. Suniti sees yet another image of saint in a vision. She sees a saint working with perfection like a Robot feeding the hungry, clothing the poor and tending the wounded on a battlefield. But this robot like perfection is an unattainable ideal for her. She, therefore, notes:

> A saint is a clod, a robot.
> A saint is what
> I clearly am not.
>
> (*SS* 16)

She badly needs a different dream. Then she sees the luminous saintly world where everything is beaming in unison. Overawed, she flees searching for a less alien scene.

Then Suniti comes up with a flash like realization that trees must be saints. They clothe the poor and feed the hungry. They are beautiful, graceful, loving and contented. She shares her revelation with her neighbour, but when the latter relentlessly lists out shrubs, creepers, smaller plants, daisies and so on for consideration of canonization, Suniti quickly withdraws her proposition.

A well meaning friend advises Suniti to set up as a saint in order to become one. After all, poets and dentists too become professionals through practice. Suniti flings herself on a nearby tree stump and stares into space trying to look a saint. A woman, whose son is hanged for murder, throws herself at Suniti's feet. Suniti merely nods at her and answers all her questions in affirmative. The poor woman is relieved, the well-meaning friend is reassured, but Suniti feels terrible. The next day a fellow expatriate suggests that Suniti should turn a poet to become a saint. After all Eknath, Tukaram and Mira Bai are all poets. Suniti on further reflection decides: "I feel I have a better chance of being a good poet than of being a good person" (*SS* 21).

The manuscript breaks off periodically to admit jottings from the War Diary of Suniti. These refer to contemporary political events such as the bombing of Israel in 1991, the killings of the Iraqi soldiers and large scale destruction of human life. In the context of such violence and mass killings the very attempt of becoming a saint appears incongruous. Evil now appears substantial and looms large, unconquered and ubiquitous to Suniti. War, death and destruction are neither visions nor images but real; and the suffering and pain of soldiers falling dead in the field is no artist's imagination either. The young men and women who lose their life in war and violence do not become martyrs or St. Georges, but their death is as significant as that of a saint or a martyr.

Suniti then tries to comprehend the nature of this substantial evil by confronting the devil. Then she realizes that there is a kinship between the devil and human beings. A war is not fought between the devil and the humans, but a devil and humans fight another devil and other humans on the other side. This realization makes her sad and depressed. Both devil and human beings are creatures and neither is really intent on committing evil. Namjoshi inserts her reflections on war into the narrative here. Poets who fought in the wars are called 'war poets'. But what about the people who lived through a war and didn't fight it? As a woman and a poet living through the wars fought by women, is she too a war poet?

At this point as Namjoshi resumes the narrative, Suniti's quest for sainthood gets subtly transformed into a search for the devil. In the manner of the Genesis incident, Suniti meets the devil in serpent form in a garden. She first picks up a twig in an attempt to attack the serpent but quickly realizes that such an attempt is futile; she then thinks of a clever play and brings a saucer of milk for the serpent. While the serpent sips milk, Suniti tries making a pact with the serpent: "be my friend. I acknowledge you now. Live with me secretly. Bite my enemies. Teach me your skills. And for all the evil that we do take your half-share. Or, indeed – my share as well" (*SS* 27). The serpent is shocked by the cunning of humans and quickly slips away without a word.

Suniti then decides that the garden-snake is no devil at all. She, therefore, thinks of putting an advertisement in the paper seeking partnership with a devil. But why will the devil befriend her? She wants the devil after all to share the blame. Suniti, then realizes that being good is difficult but trying to be evil not any easier.

The whole question of good and evil becomes superfluous in the context of larger crises that affect human lives; In fact prose, verse, all forms of expression becomes useless to talk about such things as famine in Africa, cyclone in Bangladesh, the plight of the Kurds etc. Namjoshi asks in a moment of utter helplessness: "Why has it happened? Why do things happen over and over and over again?" (*SS* 30). Life doesn't happen in ways that can be enclosed in a poem. The poet in her begins to wonder:

> Is there something inherently indecent about trying to write verse?
>
> (*SS* 31)

Namjoshi thus deals with a stock literary theme – conflict between good and evil -- in a completely unconventional manner. Suniti who aspires for sainthood realizes that she needs to slay the dragon of evil in order to merit canonization. But the real revelation comes when she realizes that evil after all is no monster, dragon or demon as she had all along imagined but ubiquitous. The entire literary tradition from *Beowulf*, for instance, created demons and dragons and projected them as incarnations of evil. The heroes and saints emerge through their combats with dragons. But all these paradigms are imaginary, and in actuality evil is a construct created by humans and humans are a part of this creation, themselves.

What is remarkable here is the author's penchant for levity and playfulness even while handling serious philosophical themes. The self-conscious narrator indulges in a mockery of reality, flouts conventions, parodies literary texts as well as conventions of the past.

* * *

"The Solidarity Fables" constitute the second half of *Saint Suniti and the Dragon* and these fables deal with a variety of issues such as power relations, social systems, cultural and literary conventions, trajectories of revolutionary movements etc. The title is ironic and the stories are not so much about solidarity as the lack of it. Namjoshi's irony gains a sharper edge in these fables but her vision emerges more enigmatic. This may be so because her preoccupation in this set of fables is essentially with concepts and her objective is to effect a transformation at the conceptual level. She raises difficult questions about good and evil, civility and rusticity, ordinary and extraordinary, patriarchy, power and domination through subtle inversions of stereotypes, juxtaposition of the contraries, witty word play and an interesting interplay of images.

Some of the fables in this collection express her disappointment with the replication of patriarchal power hierarchy in feminist groups. In the "Lost Leader" she makes fun of the elitist hedgehog who takes upon herself the responsibility of civilizing vulgar hedgehogs on proper social graces and "enlighten them". The hedgehog hosts a meeting and offers a feast of delicate flowers and bunches of grapes and tries to educate "vulgar hedgehogs" by telling them that hedgehogs are wonderful and enjoy best things in life. The motley group grabs, grunts and falls upon the food. Horrified, the leader shouts: "It is time we came out". The crowd streams out of the gate on to the streets jostling and pushing away the hostess. Finally, the refined hedgehog does go down in history not as she had intended but as "the legendary leader and first casualty of the hedgehog cause". This is how often martyrs are made in popular revolutions.

"That Shaggy Look" is about the enthusiasm of a young revolutionary to turn every thing into a ritual and a cult. The wild mare who had moved to the moors lived there for long and almost forgot why she had originally moved out. But the young enthusiasts appropriate her as a cult figure for their revolution, and attribute ideological postures to her. Her young niece asks her why she had moved to the moors and answers the question herself: "It was because you were fed up with bourgeoisie respectability and creature comforts, wasn't it?" (*SS* 60). Then she assumes that the wild mare's shaggy look is a form of her protest. The wild mare to her utter dismay realizes that she has gained a strange reputation, the reputation of a tourist attraction. In short delightful tales Namjoshi ridicules the excesses of revolution and warns the enthusiasts against the possibility of turning avantgarde into establishment and diluting the revolutionary potential of the movement.

Alongside there are also stories about patriarchal domination and gender discrimination. For instance, "Bluebeard's Way" is about a miser who hoards gold, furniture and women as well. He looks after women as carefully as one would his milch cows and prospers. Bluebeard's way becomes the way of living for generations though some mutations and transmutations occur in the philosophy in course of time. One of the worst mutations is, women who themselves constitute property are allowed to own property. This liberates them and the result is chaos. Some Bluebeards continue to insist: "Authority and territory are the Right of Man" (*SS* 101), and hope that the world would return to the fundamentals.

Nowhere is patriarchy more strongly asserted than in the moral tales of the past. For instance, there are stories about the wicked wolves who harass young maidens almost in all literatures. Namjoshi's 'Wolf' is an attack on stereotyping creatures. The wicked wolf is, after all, a construct created to let the young men emerge as heroes. But if the maidens were to make friends with wolves, then the heroes become redundant. "Subsequent History" shows how the newly found friendship between the woman and the wolf is popularly detested. This is understandable: if two oppressed groups come together the oppressor feels threatened.

A number of stories in this set deal with power relations and point to the fact that all forms of domination ultimately boil down to the question of power. In "Pelican", for instance, the fish are willing to consider pelicans fellowfish; but the question is: Will pelicans consider their prey fellow beings? "Gracefully for Grebes" is about grebes scared by a giant crab with a sign on its back "I eat grebes". Grebes eat crabs but are not used to the idea of Grebe-eating crabs. This sudden reversal dismays them, and they quickly sue for peace with the crab, promising that they would never attack any crustacean that is "superior in size". The eater-eaten relationship, after all, is a replication in nature of the relationship between the powerful and the powerless.

In "The Promise of King Hilar", Namjoshi inverts the stock rescue situation wherein damsels in distress are saved by heroes, and makes an old woman in the forest rescue the king who falls off his horse and sprains his ankle. The king insists that he should reward the woman suitably. Totally ignorant of the kind of life the old woman lives in the forest and unmindful of her preference, the king offers her the choice of two black elephants, two riding camels and one thoroughbred horse. The old woman declines the presents since none of them is of any use to her. Moreover they would be a burden on her meagre means. The monarch insists she ask for something, and therefore she requests the king to make her a cup of tea. After a great deal of effort the king produces a cup of weak tea. King Hilar in this story signifies the blindness of the affluent and the powerful, to the everyday realities of life around them.

Namjoshi also plays with literary conventions and deliberately deconstructs them in order to free poetic imagination from frigid patterns of thought. In "Art is Long etc." she twists the familiar adage 'Art is long and life is short' out of shape to assert the importance of life over everything else. "Beauty Incarnate and the Supreme Singer" is a spoof on the conventions of romantic poetry. Self-sacrificing and suffering lover singing plaintive notes to his heartless beloved is ridiculed here. "Calvin Versus Darwin Versus the Pelican" is a playful dig at all kinds of theological and scientific dogmatism. The moralist here argues that the penguin is an instance of the dire consequences of giving way to a slothful impulse, and adds that penguins have lost their power to fly on account of centuries of sloth and become congenitally indolent. He hardly finishes the discourse when the penguin returns flying gracefully through the waves on her adaptable fins.

Namjoshi often raises serious and important questions in a

casual and jovial tone. She reframes the philosophic question 'can we separate dance from the dancer?' in her story "The Guitar Player". The guitarist is a young girl courted by two lovers who come to her lured by her music. But when asked: "Is it me you love or my guitar?" (*SS* 74), they fail to come up with the expected simple answer – they love her all together.

The concepts of ordinary and extraordinary are exposed as matters of mere projection and perception in Namjoshi's tales. For instance, red birds with two green wings pass off for rare birds in the forest, since they look different from the rest and they manage to project their difference as their distinction. Finally, the zoologist who comes to the forest declares that they are as ordinary as any other birds in the forest, and uniqueness is exposed as an acquired reputation. In "Ordinary Ears" a mother sow gives birth to seven little piglets with bright red ears. When the eighth one is born with perfectly ordinary ears, she feels so disappointed that she conjures up a story that the ordinary ears of the eighth one in fact are made of pure durable silk. Her sister perpetuates the lie adding that her own little ones too have silken ears and that it must run in the family. Both the sisters feel proud that they come of "good stock". The need felt by the parent to project her offspring as special and distinguished is ridiculed in this story.

There are stories about living as an outsider in an alien land. In "Schooling" a red fish with blue dots is generally considered absurd in the company of grey fish. The red fish feels ridiculous and wonders if she could change her appearance. But the grey fish point out that it would be dishonest to do so. The red fish realizes that she would either have to be bad and beautiful or ugly and honest. It is a no-win situation for her since she is going to remain an alien in any case. "Higher Education" is about a hippo in a duck pond. The ducks with the best of intentions try to advise the hippo about how to conduct herself, but only manage to confuse her so thoroughly that she eventually disappears into the cam. The ducks conclude that the hippo had after all failed to "fit in".

"Blood and Water" one of the most powerful tales in this selection, deals with the mother-daughter relationship. When the disobedient daughters of the River Ganga diverge publicly and prove deviant and opt to follow their own course, their mother changes them all into pale blue flowers and sends them away to live "undistinguished, unhonoured and unashamed". The daughters of Ganga move out and spread across the earth. In course of time, Ganga loses her place of prime importance. The goddess Ganga falls on bad times. The daughters of Ganga hear the news, return to their birth place and offer to help their mother. They find their mother pleading for death with the last of her passions. Once they see death approach, "With a sound like the shattering of millions upon millions of glass petals, the Daughters of Ganga flooded the riverbed" (*SS* 90).

Most stories in this set underscore the need for female bonding on terms of equality and mutual understanding. Namjoshi comments upon the internal divisions, controversies and recriminations that created a backlash within the feminist movement and stresses the need for 'solidarity'. Messages are not given directly (moralization and preaching have never been Namjoshi's method of articulation or communication) but hinted at in witty and paradoxical parables and fables. Genial humour and gentle irony inform all these stories and the writer's genuine concern for the existing state of affairs in society in general and women's movements in particular is inscribed in each of these tragi-comic tales.

Works Cited

Arendt, Hannah. *The Human Condition*. Chicago: University of Chicago Press, 1958.

Freud, Sigmund. *Beyond the Pleasure Principle*. Trans. James Strachey. New York: Norton, 1961.

Namjoshi, Suniti. *Because of India*. London: Only Women's Press, 1989.

—. *The Blue Donkey Fables. The Mothers of Maya Diip*. New Delhi: Penguin, 1991.

—. *Saint Suniti and The Dragon*. London: Virago, 1994.

Ostriker, Alicia. "The Thieves of Language: Women Poets and Revisionist Mythmaking." *The New Feminist Criticism: Essays on Women, Literature and Theory*. Ed. Elaine Showalter. New York: Pantheon Books, 1985.

Yaegar, Patricia. *Honey-Mad Women*. New York: Columbia University Press, 1988.

7

Readerfriendly Text: *Building Babel*

Namjoshi has always preferred to leave her texts open for multiple readings. Even as she reread the canonical texts – Shakespeare's *The Tempest*, Ovid's *Metamorphosis*, Vishnu Sarma's *Panchatantra* or Anderson's Fables, she has obviously maintained that texts are meant to be read, and re-reàd differently and variously. Implied in such a position is the assumption that the reader is no passive recipient of meaning, but an active participant in the making of meanings. Namjoshi's constant preoccupation with the process of poetic communication, the respective roles of the writer and reader and, nature of literary composition is reflected in the increasingly metatextual content of her recent work. Considering this, it is only natural that she should come up with her version of an interactive text in her latest work *Building Babel*.

This idea connects well with the concept of meaning as a

participatory event in the oral literary traditions of India. There are no fixed texts, but texts are constantly reinterpreted as they are passed on from one narrator to another. There are, for instance, several interpretations of the Upanishadic texts. As Namjoshi herself aptly sums up: "Every re-telling of myth is a re-working of it. Every hearing or reading of a myth is a re-creation of it. It is only when we engage with a myth that it resonates, that it becomes charged and re-charged with meaning" (*BB*, XI).

It is interesting to recall Barthes's distinction between readable/readerly and writable/writerly (or lisible/scriptible) texts in this context. While readable text is defined as that which is serious, fixed, closed, structural, constrained, authoritarian and unitary, the writable text is playful, fluid, open, plural, and opposed to the repressive rule of structure, grammar or logic (*S/Z* 6). Readable text is systematic, the writable mocks all attempts at systematization. In Barthes's analysis, a writable text elicits from the reader/critic not commentary but *jouissance*. Namjoshi's *Building Babel* is a writable text by Barthes's criteria, but it invites the readers not only to partake of the pleasures of text, but to un-write and rewrite the text in their own way. *Building Babel* defies all traditional criteria of readability such as linearity, coherence, consistency, credibility and convincing characterization. It, therefore, cannot be analysed or critically interpreted. In fact it is not meant for such an exercise. Therefore the discussion of the text that follows resists the temptation to reorder and rationalize the fragment into a cohesive "story", since such a reading might erase or repress those aspects of the text which make it new, experimental and subversive. Instead, the commentary offered here focuses on the plurality of meanings intended by the author and avoids conclusive observations.

The central symbol of the novel is Babel and it denotes culture. *Building Babel* is all about the process of building culture. Building culture is seen as a continuous process where every one participates, constantly makes, unmakes and remakes and as Cinders, one of the characters in the novel, puts it: "It's the building of the building that *is* the project" (*BB*, 34). Culture is not the product of a process but it is the process itself: it is not static or fixed at any point of time, but is constantly changing and eternally evolving. The novel narrates this process of building culture which takes place under the aegis of Crone Kronos or Time. Namjoshi invents Crone Kronos for the purposes of building Babel just the same way gods are invented in the Hindu pantheon. Crone Kronos is Time or mystery of life and existence, and making stories about the mystery is a way to apprehend it. Making stories becomes the objective correlative of building culture (or Babel), and when the readers are finally invited to take part in the process, the story is handed over to them.

The characters in the novel -- Little Red, Sister Solitude, Black Piglet, Rap Rap, Cinders, Alice, Snow White, Rose Green, and the three Gorgons – Mad med, Verity and Charity, are all recreations of familiar characters from the past. They have something of their old *avatar* in them and they also have a new identity here. Each one of them is connected diachronically to a literary ancestor of the past and synchronically to a category of contemporary women. For instance, Namjoshi's Little Red is a recreation of Red Ridinghood, and is also comparable to Chaucer's the Wife of Bath. Little Red is however, "less raucous, more seemly" (*BB* 1). The likes of Little Red may be found in a ranch in America, a station in Australia, or any city in India. Sister Sol, on the other hand, is "severe, savage and suggestible." Her literary ancestry is not as clearly traceable as that of Little Red. Namjoshi likens her to Olivia "who lacks commonsense, both proud and needy" (*BB* 2). Sweet Sister Sols are a common species found by the dozens and millions.

The Black Piglet is "a voyager, a wanderer and a thinker". The identity of the Black Piglet is particularly perplexing. It is the prince turned into a pig by the arch sorceress, Circe. The Black Piglet constantly changes its form and assumes different identities at different points of time. It is prince at times, princess on occasions, and a piglet most of the time. She plays a vital role in building Babel. She is also a storyteller, a dreamer given to contemplation. She has no fixed place or class but lives chiefly inside her head and quite enjoys it. Rap Rap is, of course, Rapunzel, and she is a well-dressed woman, proper and perfect in everything. She is able, ambitious and is an achiever. Cinders, is the new incarnation of Cinderella who has leapt from rags to riches. The transformation was easy: the prince had it all, and she had the prince.

Alice is a recreation of Queen Alice from Lewis Carroll's novel and possesses all the power and charm of the original in *Through the Looking Glass*. She likes to control and is perfect at exercising power. The Villain – Villainess is a scheming "creator who had nothing and therefore wanted everyone's anything" (*BB* 5). Lady Shy is the most heartful of them all, but fails to get the attention she deserves either due to bad PR or bad *karma*. The minor characters include Snow White and Rose Green who are typical college students, same everywhere, and the cat which is very much like Alice's Cat. Then there are the three Gorgons: Mad Med, Verity and Charity. Sister Charity is 'sweet, sickly and apparently unlikable'. Verity's singular strength is in her name and Mad Med is all blood and guts. "These are the characters. They are pilgrims all" – This is how Namjoshi introduces them to her readers. They are all sisters engaged in building Babel and interrelations, interconnections and interactions place them in an intricate network.

In the world of Babel, all accepted notions of time, power and discipline of love come under scrutiny. In fact, it begins with sisters analysing the very notions of sisterhood. For instance two sisters – Snow White and Rose Green – tell each other lies and fabricate histories. But their sisterhood stops short of perfection as one of them says: "I would like to be the boss of the whole planet and have it solely for me" (*BB* 10). This idiom of power and monopoly renders sisterhood an impossible ideal. Sisterhood in such an analysis becomes a mere pact of mutual convenience and benefit, and a polarization of forces against a common enemy. Sister Solitude seeks sisterhood with the moon, the frog, and lily but receives no assent. Alice likes to have sisterhood with the cat, but the latter is suspicious of bonding with someone so different. Can different beings retain their 'difference' and still be equal? Black Piglet, the visionary and the idealist realizes that the only soul mate one can find is one's death. Thus each one of the characters is engaged in interrogating received notions of identity and social relationships.

The need for building babel is felt intensely by the sisters as they realize that they are all imprisoned in the tales of past in one way or the other. Cinders (Cinderella) Rap Rap (Rapunzel), Little Red are trapped in the tales of the past. Their behaviour, their appearance, their fate is all determined by the discourse in which they are locked up. For instance, Little Red hates being red, and complains that she has been stereotyped. They all realize that they have all been typecast. This leads to the insight that the real problem is neither God nor man but language. It is words that make worlds and words need to be reinvented if the world and world view are to be transformed. So they decide to "build a great edifice out of malleable words", "cultivate a culture" and "grow a common language" (*Building Babel* 29). Only then will sisterhood mean something.

Building Babel is an important activity as it enables sisters develop a sense of interconnectedness. Rap Rap is to be the architect, Little Red would find a suitable site and Cinders is to deal with permissions and licenses. Even loners like Sister Solitude get involved in the process. The Black Piglet does the mountainous task of sorting out various things piled up as a part of the process of Babel building. Building Babel, however, is a hazardous task and a number of questions and challenges crop up from time to time. In fact, the various participants in the project are not sure of what exactly they are building. Some of them indulge in storytelling and by making stories about Crone Kronos they make Crone Kronos.

The most important problem the builders of Babel face is to find a language that can capture time and reality which are forever changing. A number of important issues such as fluidity of identity, multiplicity of perceptions and meanings, paradoxes of language and expression come under scrutiny in the playful exchanges of ideas and wit that the sisters engage in. What is particularly interesting in this regard is Namjoshi's method of asking serious questions in an apparently frivolous tone, and pushing the readers into the game of asking questions and guessing possible answers. In fact it is not important to find satisfactory answers, it is more important to ask questions. Perpetual enquiry and exploration motivate building babel which in effect is an eternal process.

Even though the sisters begin the building of babel in a mood of solidarity and sisterhood, they soon fall into factions and a power struggle ensues in the world of Babel. There are coups and counter coups and the early leaders of Babel building, Black Piglet and Solitude are challenged by the revolutionaries. Lady Shy (Shakespeare's Jew in a mutated form) espouses the cause of working sisters and opposes the elitism of the leaders of Babel. She insists that Babel has not risen to the tuneful taletelling of a few, but was built by the sweat and blood of a multitude of women (*BB* 62). Thus the class struggle breaks out and the divide between thinkers and activists surfaces. As Namjoshi portrays the civil strife among sisters, she is obviously referring to the backlash within the feminist movement. Fractions, divisions and differences are a part of evolution. Memes, after all mutate, and mutation ensures continuation. Change, mutation, perpetual erasure and re-writing constitute the essence of Babel building.

In the newly-built world of sisters, the questions of power and authority re-emerge albeit in an altered form. The old guard actually involved in building babel are eased out and a new dispensation under Queen Alice is ushered in. Hierarchy, domination and exploitation – the ills of patriarchy against which the sisterhood was formed are back in this new world of all women. When Queen Alice takes charge of the Babel, the first thing she does is to establish a power base and place herself at the apex of that power hierarchy. She lays down the channels of power and makes herself the source of power. A myth of good queen Alice is set in circulation, and allegiance to the Queen is carefully cultivated and the Queen's rule is established.

Monarchy, monopoly and class system are resurrected in the world of all women. Another question that vexes the Builders of Babel is the 'man's question'. How are men to be treated? Should they be permitted entry into the world of Babel or not? What should be their status in the new dispensation? Arguments for and against are aired, debates held and opinions differed. Males are finally let in mainly as immigrants. They occupy an inferior position but may achieve the status of a woman through toil and dedication to the ideals of Babel. Women of Babel indulge in playful dalliance with them, and it is not considered an offence at all, since men are meant to be the objects of pleasure. Obviously here is an inversion of what goes an in the male dominated world, only the gender roles are reversed.

Namjoshi does not consider gender-role inversion a viable solution to the existing gender conflicts. She denounces the polarization of male vs female as a recreation of a heterosexual dispensation. Identity as Namjoshi repeatedly points out is neither fixed nor absolute. It is fluid and changing. Greeks may call it metamorphosis and Hindus consider the notion of metempsychosis. Namjoshi favours an identity which is under constant change and she is particularly happy with the possibility of changing from one form to another. For instance, Black Piglet when unveiled becomes black Prince and assumes the form of a princess as well. Namjoshi's Rabbit sounds like her author's mouthpiece when he/she/it wishes:

> I want to go back to that lost forest
> where metaphors mix,
> rub shoulders with each other,
> And everything turns to everything else.
>
> (*BB* 168)

Nothing remains stable in the tower of Babel: Queen Alice grows old and the baronesses of Babel fight each other to seize the source of power. After the death of Alice, chaos is let loose and a civil war breaks out. Violence, bloodshed and homicide mark the place. Well, all this is done in the name of Babel, the glory of womanhood, the beauty of nationhood, and the gorgeousness of peoplehood! The Cat who narrates the story of Queen Alice concludes on a note of resignation: "Babel was no longer distinguishable from any other city. Perhaps it would disintegrate, perhaps not. Who cared?" (*BB* 140).

In the next phase the site of Babel building is shifted to Mad Medusa. There are memes she inherited from her sisters, and each time she scrabbles through the memes a different story is made. Then she realizes that Babel may be built even when she sits still and lets memes take their own shapes. After all "culture does not require cultivation" (*BB* 153-154). In fact all of us have something of Mad Medusa in us, and we contribute to the process of building Babel intentionally or otherwise.

It is not hard to guess why Namjoshi chooses Medusa as one of the key figures in the making of Babel. The figure alludes both to the Greek myth and to Freud's reading of it. According to the Ovidian myth, the Gorgon Medusa was once beautiful, "the hope of many an envious suitor," until one day Neptune raped her in Minerva's temple – where upon the Goddess outraged turned Medusa into a monster. Ovid also narrates how the hero Perseus severed Medusa's head and how "from that mother's bleeding/Were born the swift-winged Pegasus and his brother" (1955: 106). The Gorgon's head thereafter became a powerful weapon turning all those (men) who looked at it into stone. Freud read the decapitated Medusa's head as a symbol of mother's castrated genitals seen from the terrorized point of view of the male spectator. Medusa, the much abused figure in male discourse, comes in for a retrieval in feminist writing. Helene Cixous's "The Laugh of the Medusa" is one of the most powerful re-writings of the myth of Medusa. In Cixous's revision, Medusa is restored to her beautiful state as before the rape and her head invites the attention of men and women rather than aversion. The laughing Medusa of Cixous as Susan Suleiman points out, "becomes a trope for women's autonomous subjectivity and for the necessary irreverence of women's writing – and rewriting" (1990: 168). Namjoshi's Medusa is the keeper of memes, and plays a vital role in creating a new culture, in building Babel.

Mad Medusa inherits building blocks from her ancestors – early builders of Babel. Now it is her turn to put them together, to make whatever words she wants to. "Mad Medusa, raped by Poseidon, betrayed by Athene, slaughtered with the aid of her own powers, surely the stupidest woman on earth examines what is left" (*BB* 141). Each letter of the alphabet stands for innumerable words and these words may be assembled in infinite ways in building Babel. Medusa is, in fact, perplexed by the range of possibilities available to her. She scrabbles through the memes, conjures up Sister Charity and Verity and makes up stories about them. Not content with their reciprocity, she decides she needs men, since "men can be a load of fun." There are no men in Babel, and she petitions Crone Kronos and demands: "If you want me to play with the memes of Babel, I must have my Man" (*BB* 147).

The Black Piglet presents herself to Med in the form of the Black Prince. Medusa indulges in an amorous play with the prince, and then realizes she cannot "spend all her time on pretty toy boys". She must perform; she must build Babel and build better than all her ancestors. She makes tales about building Babel, but her version is constantly countered by the early builders – Cinders, Rap Rap and Little Red. An annoyed Medusa decides to kill her ancestors whatever she might come to pass. She makes another version of the story of Babel building, in which a man scorns at all the sisters of Babel and tells them "Babel wasn't built by the gossip of women. – The building of Babel requires brute strength" (*BB* 152). Medusa realizes that a story about how they (sisters) didn't build Babel is also a story about the building of it (*BB* 153). She then decides to remain inactive and let the Babel make itself. After all "culture does not require cultivation." Medusa then thinks of Queen Alice, and her subsequent speculations have interesting intertextual references to 'A Mad Tea Party' in Lewis Carroll's *Alice in Wonderland*. Med and Alice play with memes, play with words, ideas, images and build Babel, "They build Babel. They do what they like. They do what they can. They do not do very well. They try again" (BB 157).

Alice and Med make stories of different kinds of life. In the first version, they conceive earthly paradise where everyone and everything get on with each other. Every one has the same power, every one is an individual and every one is healthy and goes on for ever. But there is a problem here. Like in the Paradise there is the individual will. If one chooses to fall, then it cannot be averted. In another version they think of life on earth in which Alice becomes the power behind the Throne. She amasses all wealth and plays the benevolent parent. Med becomes the poet, historian and thinker living on the grants sanctioned by the Alice Foundation! In the next movement, they imagine life in eternity. In eternity Crone Kronos fills and envelops everything, and one is absorbed by the all pervasive principle of Time.

The next section titled "Patched Piece" is marked by an

orchestration of multiple voices – All the sisters engage in a retrospective analysis of the process of building Babel. It is Mad Med who comes up with the discovery that "Babel cannot bloom in the desert air, and that a text doesn't exist until it's read". The gates of Babel are then thrown open to one and all.

In the final section called "The Reader's Text", the writer establishes a direct contact with the reader and invites the reader to contribute to the building of Babel. The author inscribes a reader who questions, revolts and at times refuses to join Babel Building. However the fact of the matter is, as Medusa puts it, the reader is complicit. In the act of reading he/she inevitably builds. Namjoshi hands over her text to the readers completely by placing the last chapter of her book on the web open for mutations, transmutations, multiple readings and re-writings. The distinction between the narratee and the narrator, reader and the scriptor is thus predictably eliminated. The reader becomes the scriptor inventing his/her own version of the story and inscribing it in cyberspace.

In this novel Namjoshi has achieved a rare feat: she has given us a narrative as rich and complex as that of building babel itself. A brief reference to the narrative strategies Namjoshi selects to reach out to her readers is in order here. The reader in Namjoshi's fabulist fiction is not merely a recipient, a passive listener. Through the dynamics of the novel, he/she is directly involved in the process of figuring out the meaning of the text by putting together and assessing different elements. The fractured structure of the novel fosters a rich diversity of reading experiences and in contrast to didactic impulse so common in fabular/utopian fiction, invites readers to make multiple meanings. The text is prefaced with two introductions by the author, and the section that follows is titled 'Prologue/Epilogue' reminding the reader of the possibility that the end may well be found in the beginning. Then there is a piece for soloists and the next major section is a biography of the black piglet as recorded by Sister Solitude.

Solitude's narrative, however, is constantly interrogated and modified by other characters in the novel. While Chapter III is an interlude, Chapter IV is an account of the reign of Queen Alice, the narrator being Alice's Cat. Mad Med's story is told by the author and "Patched Piece" that follows records multiple voices. The last chapter is aptly called "Reader's Text" as it is an invitation to the readers to take over the baton of narration. Even as the narrators indulge in detailed account of places, peoples and incidents, there is a subtle undercutting of reality in the midst of precise detail. No single perspective, narrative tone or even generic approach guides the reader. The book is a collage of stories, dialogues, poems and myths, and celebrates the dynamic and fluid culture central to the feminist babel.

Namjoshi encourages reader involvement through her discontinuous structure. Although there is a central event in the novel -- building of babel -- there is no single central narrative. It is constantly interpolated and the readers piece together the fragments. Although at first different sections seem unrelated, in the reading process one will discover multiple connections both large and small. Explicitly and implicitly, the discontinuous, multigenred narrative structure demands that the reader make meaning. Namjoshi, in fact, works on her readers in a variety of ways. Abundant invention and deconstruction, multiple fictional frames, generic diversity -- all these strategies demand active reading. Whether as readers we are invited, cajoled, teased or left hanging and forced to pick up the pieces, we are definitely involved.

Direct address is frequent and varies from an invitation to participate to an insistence on the importance of the vital connection between the narrator and the readers. In the last section the narrator announces: "we could rip off our masks" and comes out to make friends with the readers directly. Then she cajoles the reader in the words of one of her characters Medusa: "Dear Reader, Sweet Barbarian, don't you understand that you *are* complicit? In the act of reading you inevitably build" (*BB* 190). My own reading of the text in this chapter is only one possible way of looking at the text and the Babel is open for multiple readings and each readings is in turn a part of Babel building!

Even as Namjoshi transgresses the logic of traditional narrative, she structures her narrative according to an analysable code quite logical according to its own norms. There are many narrators here, but the three major narrators are (i) the author (ii) Sisters Solitude and (iii) Cat C. The author is the omniscient narrator in many parts of the story; the story of Black Piglet is set down as a chronicle written by Sister Solitude; Queen Alice's story is told from the perspective of Cat. However, the narrative often slides from one narrative voice to another, from one time and place sequence to another. For instance, Sister Solitude's chronicle is cluttered with asides, contradictory comments, objections put in by other characters. The chronicle is constantly modified and modulated by these interpolations. The effect of these interventions is to de-realize the fiction and to insert the problem of reading of the text into the very space of its unfolding.

Namjoshi's *Building Babel* is a striking instance of counter discourse as it deliberately breaks all convention of realism and realistic narrative and celebrates inconsistencies and contradictions. Realism as a mode of narrative reflects a belief in the principle of noncontradiction, in temporal succession and causality, in the solidity of objects and in the unity of self. "The realist novel" as Susan Suleiman rightly points out "invites readers to make sense of it in a way that is not essentially different from the way they try to make sense of the world around them" (1990: 35). In rejecting realism, Namjoshi rejects all the ontological presuppositions that go with it and breaks the criteria of narrative intelligibility. Instead, she offers the readers apparently random events, contradictory versions of reality, disembodied voices and fragmented narrative. The reader has both the freedom and the function to make his/her own inferences, and consequently each reader constructs his/her own version of the story. Thus Namjoshi creates a communicative and interactive text in *Building Babel* and draws on cyber resources for developing a network of communication in which the writer and the readers become co-authors in scripting a never-ending story. Story telling is analogous to building culture and both these processes are coeval with human existence.

Works Cited

Barthes, Roland. *S/Z*. Trans. Richard Miller. New York: Hill and Wang, 1974.

Cixous, Helene. "The Laugh of the Medusa". Trans. Keith Cohen and Paula Cohen. In *New French Feminisms*. Ed. Elaine Marks and Isabelle de Courtivron. Amherst: University of Massachusetts Press, 1980. 245-264.

Namjoshi, Suniti. *Building Babel*. Melbourne: Spinifex, 1996.

Ovid. *Metamorphoses*. Trans. Rolfe Humphrises. Bloomington: Indiana University Press, 1955.

Suleiman, R. Susan. *Subversive Intent: Gender, Politics, and the Avant-Garde*. Cambridge: Harvard University Press, 1990.

8

In/Conclusion

This study has identified fluidity and inconclusiveness as the distinctive features of Namjoshi's writing. Therefore, any attempt to offer conclusive observations will go against the very thesis of this argument. Moreover, one should not hope to make definitive statements about a living writer's work which in effect is work in progress. I shall merely highlight what to me are the most fascinating aspects of Namjoshi's poetry and fiction that find her a secure place among contemporary writers.

I have tried to locate Namjoshi's work within the context of some the recent developments in narrative and theoretical practice. From my readings Namjoshi primarily emerges as an allegorical fabulator. In her work, ideation and fiction are inextricably intertwined. She is in quest of alternatives to the existing modes of being, and fantasy and irony are her instruments in negotiating possibilities. While fantasy enables her to construct an unreal world from the specifics of the real, irony equips her with a means to negate the truth and validity of a received tradition. Neither irony nor fantasy is governed by rules of right and wrong, truth and falsity; instead they bring all rigid and fixed structures of thought and ideation under interrogation. Namjoshi presses into service the subversive potential of these devices to play with patriarchal norms, hegemonic structures, familial and sexual codes as well as literary and generic conventions.

What Namjoshi's entire work – poems, fables and novels – taken together conveys clearly is a strong resistance to the status quo of oppression be it gender based, race based or class based. Transgression, not so much aggression, is her mode of articulating resistance. Her work re-writes all social constructions including subjectivity, sexuality and gender.

Textual transgressions in Namjoshi's work are actually meant to urge the need for a cognitive and perceptual transformation. The polemic in her work never becomes obvious; instead a mood of playfulness and mirth pervades her texts.

Even as Namjoshi's stresses the need for a revision – a radical revision – of existing systems and situations, she does not offer a single viable alternative to substitute what she demolishes through subversion. On the contrary, she deliberately produces ambivalence as a textual strategy and involves readers in an active quest for plural possibilities. This quest is more in the form of a shared game in which the author and reader co-operate, and it is a continual process rather than achievement of stasis. Namjoshi texts, therefore, move beyond endings and eschew closures. It is profitable to recall Helene Cixous's description of a feminine text in this context. According to Cixous, a feminine text "is always endless, without ending: there's no closure, it does not stop ..." (1976: 53).

Namjoshi's work as anti-canonical counter discourse is a significant experiment in postcolonial and feminist writing. Through a successful subversion of canonical texts/genres, she rewrites the master narratives, erases the distinction between prose and verse, dethrones the textual authority and liberates the objects of the imperial/patriarchal discourse. Namjoshi's work announces a textual revolt opposing and decentering the dominant discourse from within and, achieves a major breakthrough in feminist/postcolonial writing. To date critical response to Suniti Namjoshi's work has been limited to reviews of her books and brief articles on isolated texts. As the first full-length study of Namjoshi's work this study, it is hoped, would serve as a useful introduction to a dynamic and complex writer whose work invites and sustains multiple readings.

Work Cited

Cixous, Helenè. "Castration or Decapitation?" Trans. Annette Kuhn. *Signs*. 7.1 (Summer 1976): 41-55.

9

Goja: A Postscript

The publication of Namjoshi's latest work: *Goja*, 'an autobiographical myth' as she describes it in the subtitle, shortly before the manuscript of this study was completed made it possible to include this relatively brief assessment of the text provided here. *Goja* has proved to be a work, which while enforcing many of the imperatives of Namjoshi's work discussed throughout this study, also offers a decisive analysis of her experience of living in/between two cultures and continents. Namjoshi has talked about her experience of living as an immigrant in the US, Canada and UK though obliquely in a number of her earlier works too. In fact in one of her very early poems, "Can a Body Hurt a Body?" (1971), she noted that the assimilative America has a mote in her eye. She continued to reflect on questions of identity in relation to alternate sexualilties and immigrant living in her subsequent work as well. For instance, central characters in her fantasy tales, Suniti in *The Conversations of Cow* and Jyanvi in *The Mothers of Maya Diip* are identified as immigrants and lesbians. *Goja*, however, is her first comprehensive account of her experience of inhabiting in/between spaces geographically, psychologically and sexually.

Goja is located in an in/between space in generic terms as well. The boundaries of genre never mattered much to Namjoshi; they have always been under erasure in her work. She describes *Goja* as an autobiographical myth and elaborates the generic identity of her work thus: "This account is autobiographical in that my experience is all I have. It's fiction since any version manipulates facts. And it's mythical because it's by making patterns that I make sense of all I have" (Preface to *Goja* ix). *Goja* is a retrospective reconstruction of her own life from the age of five to date by Namjoshi, but the account is not in the form of a sequential narrative. She invokes two female figures central to her childhood and growing up – Goja (her maid) and Goldie (her grandmother) – and narrates to them the story of her life. The narrative soon becomes a dialogue/conversation as Goja and Goldie do not remain silent listeners, but participate actively in the act of narration. Namjoshi's autobiography is as much about Goja and Goldie as about herself since her life is inextricably interlinked to that of these two older women who played a decisive role in her life not only as presences in her childhood but as inescapable absences in her later life outside India.

Fictional autobiography/autobiographical fiction has indeed been a popular genre with diasporic writers. Recalling one's past and recording it in a narrative to share it with readers has been an important preoccupation for writers living abroad. Writing the diaspora is a way of coming to terms with diaspora. Beginning with Santha Rama Rau's *Home to India* (1944) and *Gifts of Passage* (1961) one can recall a number of fictional autobiographies by women writers of the Indian diaspora. As Gina Whisker rightly points out; "The autobiographical mode is of particular importance to people who have been silenced hitherto" (1993: 6). Autobiography at once becomes the proof of identity and testimony to the lived experience. The last two decades have witnessed a spurt of autobiographical accounts of immigrant life by women writers: Sharanjeet Shaan's *In My Own Name* (1985), Sara Suleri's *Meatless Days* (1990), Meera Alexander's *Faultlines* (1993), Meera Syal's *Anita and Me* (1996) are some striking examples of this trend. Writing one's own life is ending one's inner silence and therefore it becomes a particularly enabling experience for diasporic writers.

Namjoshi's *Goja* may be further located in the context of lesbian autobiographies or lesbian coming-out tales. For an Indian, coming out as a lesbian in the west is very much different from publicly professing her lesbian identity in India to her family, her loved ones. It is interesting to recall Karla Jay's essay, "Coming Out as a Process" in this context. Jay emphasizes how lesbians are constantly in development, continually making that step of coming-out naming and again renaming (1978: 28-30). Namjoshi who openly came out as a lesbian more than two decades ago, continually reiterates her position in her work. In *Goja* she confesses her sexual choice to two of the significant others of her life -- her grandmother Goldie and her maid Goja both of who are dead and now textually resurrected by her. Explaining to them the factors that prompted her to leave India for good, Namjoshi says:

> I was seriously in love with a dear friend – I shall call her Sahali. She had already gone abroad and it seemed sensible to follow. By then it was clear that in India it would not be possible for two women who loved one another to live honourably together.
>
> (*Goja* 66)

She then proceeds to add:

> I took leave of Goja and my grandmother and the rest of the family and set off for the States. I did not tell them that I did not mean to return.
>
> (*Goja* 67)

What Namjoshi did not and could not tell her family then, she is putting it down in writing here, in the form of a confession to her dear ones. One of the purposes of writing this account is to reveal things about her life that she had largely kept to herself until now. "In the process of becoming a self-named lesbian," writes Betsy Warland, "every woman must find her way through a myriad fears. As she does she becomes less afraid." (1990: 123). Namjoshi gets over her fears by writing the facts of her life into this work of autobiography.

Goja may also be read as a variation on the generic model of a female *bildungsroman* or to be more specific a lesbian novel of development. It is important to note in this context that lesbian writers do not conform to conventional generic models but invent and reinvent these genres to present a literary shaping of lesbian personal politics. Bonnie Zimmerman discusses the different types of lesbian novel of development in her essay "Exiting from Patriarchy" and some of these are: the confessional, the picaresque, the portrait of the artist, the novel of awakening and the apprenticeship novel. Namjoshi's *Goja* does not fit into any of these categories but shares features with most of them. It is confessional to the extent that here Namjoshi is presenting an account of her life in the West to Goja and Goldie the most loved figures of her past; it is picaresque as it deals with her transcontinental journeys in quest of freedom and love; it traces her growth as a writer and her adventures in the woods of words; and it is about her growing awareness of what it means to be a lesbian. Like a typical lesbian hero, Namjoshi too seeks escape from the constraints of patriarchy. Escape here includes a physical journey away from the family, familiar society and identity (as the grandchild of a royal household), to the West, to anonymity and a new identity. Goja also marks a strong protest against oppressive social forces and cultural codes, which constantly pressurize an individual to adopt a role fully sanctioned by the dominant culture. Furthermore, in her characteristic manner, Namjoshi adds to her narrative, elements of fancy and myth-making forging links between the physical and the mythical. Myth is a charged term in Namjoshi's oeuvre since it provides her not merely a strategy of narration, but a mode of perception and a way of comprehension. Through myths she mediates and illuminates relationships and finds meanings in the otherwise bewildering complexity of reality.

Goja, Namjoshi's fictionalized autobiography, is not the life story of a single woman but it is about three women -- Goja, Goldie, and Suniti -- whose lives are intertwined in many ways. Namjoshi, however, chooses to name her work after Goja because the prime purpose in writing this account is to place on record her debt to her maid Goja who mothered her in her childhood. The service rendered by servants is generally taken for granted and is rarely acknowledged. Namjoshi expresses her gratitude to Goja by writing her into this book of fiction. She is also seeking Goja's forgiveness for all the wrongs the family had done to her. She knows, however, that a mere word of apology cannot set the records straight. Yet she must ask for forgiveness and hence the book. Writing about Goja, writing Goja, therefore is an act of thanksgiving an attempt at atonement. The picture of Goja that emerges from Namjoshi's account is inevitably sketchy as it is one-dimensional and only deals with Goja as seen by and as known to Namjoshi. The author tells us frankly in her opening chapter: "I don't know much about Goja. And now it's too late. Goja is gone -- I've looked for a photograph of Goja, but there are none..." *(Goja 7)*. Despite these limitations, Namjoshi's Goja dressed in a nine-yard coarse cotton sari tucked between her legs, going about a large aristocratic home attending to the needs of the family meticulously, emerges a representative figure. It could be any servant woman in any rich household in any part of India. Goja who enters the royal household as a servant at the age of five stays on with the family catering to one generation after another. Goja who feeds child Suniti dried fish in the quiet of the night, and tells her the story of crocodile, Goja who saves the prince's son and breaks her own arm, Goja who withers and shrivels into a bent old woman in the service of the Raja sahib's family is fondly recalled by Namjoshi. Goja, however silhouette-like in Namjoshi's fictional presentation, is sure to remind most readers of the silent maids who made their lives more bearable and their travails lighter.

In contrast to Goja, we have the figure of Ranisahib, Namjoshi's grandmother who dressed in rich silks, smelling of crushed flowers, presided over the household like a deity. Her role in life was to accept homage and bless lavishly and she conformed to the stereotype of Ranisahib created and upheld by the royal families. Both Goja and Goldie are part of a power structure that they can neither alter nor avoid. This power structure is rather complicated and creates different kinds of hierarchies comprising of several sets of unequal relations. Ranisahib who is worshipped as a goddess in her household occupies a dependent position in patriarchal as well as imperial structures of power. But she is privileged in her relation to Goja who only knows subordination, being a servant. Goja and Goldie play out their roles within the societal constructs of power without protesting. Namjoshi who examines their relation as well as her own relation to each of them in retrospect can clearly see the implications of power dynamics for personal lives of individuals.

Goja and Goldie provide a mirror in which Namjoshi discovers herself. She narrates to them the story of the shaping of her own lesbian identity, gives them an account of her experiences of living in anonymity abroad in a self-imposed exile, and traces for them her growth as a poet. Here Namjoshi recreates her past in a series of reminiscences focusing attention on certain nodal moments in her life. These recollections fall into three parts – 'Once in India' dealing with her childhood experiences and growing up in India; 'In Cold Canada' focusing on Namjoshi's experiences as an immigrant in Canada; 'Later' centering round her present life in England. Although the narrative is not strictly chronological or sequential, one can see the evolution of the protagonist as an individual, as a writer and as a lesbian through the experiences recalled here. However, nowhere does the narrator insist that we take what she says about herself as the ultimate truth; instead she creates her own system of internal checks and balances by letting her characters take over the narration from time to time. Besides, as Namjoshi recalls her past in a series of reminiscences, she does not merely recall the detail, but reflects on it with the knowledge she is now equipped with. For instance, Namjoshi reminisces: "I called my grandmother 'mother', but I called Goja 'Goja'. It was proper. I understand now that it was also deeply improper" (*Goja* 5). A narrative reconstitution of the past is a psychologically significant process. From the phenomenological point of view, we remember parts of the past that are still meaningful to us (Pollio 1982). As the phenomenological psychologists suggest, the importance of a remembrance is not in its accuracy in describing the past but in the interpretation we give it in the present. Remembrances are reconstructions and the autobiographical memory is a record of the past that is filtered through ones personality and current beliefs (Maslow 1954). This process of constant reviewing is at work in Namjoshi's recollections of the past.

Another important aspect of this autobiography is the deliberate mythologizing of the narrative. This, of course, is typical of Namjoshi's stories. One can never tell where reality merges into myth or vice-versa in her work. In this case the narrator invokes the Queen of Spades and the Black Piglet to serve as the points of reference and as frames of perception to raise some vital questions related to power, human relationships and morality. In a typical postmodernist strain, Namjoshi not only conjures up imaginary figures that would inhabit her fictional world, but also constantly exposes the fictionality of the so called real that is the staple of all autobiographical writing. However despite the playful demolition of all structures of reality that the writer indulges in, and her repeated warnings against the authenticity of truth, the reader can construct a fairly reliable account of Namjoshi's life from the casual factual details thrown in by the narrator in a rather cavalier fashion.

As Namjoshi recalls her early life in India, she remembers how she grew up with her grandmother and Goja while her parents spent long sojourns abroad; she distinctly remembers waiting for her parents to return to her, albeit briefly, in between their trips abroad. This waiting turned into a perpetual longing for a lost father, when her father died in a plane crash. Another nightmarish incident of her childhood that haunted her was the memory of being abused at the age of five by a servant. She was then too young to understand the violence of the act and it was much later that she realized that she had been violated and it did matter. By then she also knew that if she were to disclose what had happened to her, she "would be the one to suffer disgrace" (*Goja* 14). Namjoshi thus had understood the manipulative power of gender-based discrimination early in life. She learnt even as a schoolchild that she was "an outsider" in her own familiar society, different from the rest of the family and did not "fit in" or conform to the expectations of family and heterosexual society. Namjoshi sets down in writing her early lesbian longings and recalls the fear under which she lived in a society, which considered same sex love appalling and terrible. The pain, humiliation, and hurt she suffered silently then, finds articulation in this autobiographical account.

The second part of the text, titled 'From Cold Canada' deals with Namjoshi's experiences as an immigrant in the West. The exile brought her anonymity and a strange freedom, which comes with invisibility It did not take long for her to realize that she was both invisible and conspicuous as a brown woman in a predominantly white world. Namjoshi recalls:

> It was like being Alice in wonderland. Strange and aggressive creatures kept insisting that they were right; and any experience I had, which might have helped somehow never applied properly. (*Goja* 73)

She knew that she had little chance of changing things and learnt to cope with the problems of racism and ethnocentricity. As she looks back on those early experiences now from some temporal distance, she can see racism as not something that belonged to a particular nation or people but as one of the many manifestations of power.

Despite the problems of discrimination she had to contend with everyday, Namjoshi never considered going back home because as a lesbian she had no chance of survival at all in India. She explains:

> In the West, as a person of no importance I was unlikely to cause a scandal. And there was no family there whose glory I could tarnish. What I did or who I was didn't matter because I didn't matter.
>
> (*Goja* 75)

This freedom enabled her to live her life the way she desired as a lesbian and as a writer.

Once the major decisions in life are thus made, Namjoshi began to see more clearly that reality is perpetually manipulated and that there is no one 'Reality' but there are multiple realities. Yet another insight she developed at this time relates to the power of language. To quote Namjoshi:

> The most important thing about my encounter with the West was English language. It took me several years and required my politicization to understand how language had power over power

> itself. Over the years, Language mediated everything: my understanding of who defined whom and how effectively, my need to work out what really mattered and somehow to say it.
> (*Goja* 79)

Namjoshi therefore made language her apparatus to probe the world around her and perceive patterns in the alien world that she had chosen as her dwelling place.

As Namjoshi lived through various phases of her negotiation with the West, Goja and Goldie were always present in her mind and at each point it was important for her to imagine what they would have said or felt. Yet she couldn't tell them about her life in the West as "there was too much to say that was forbidden" (*Goja* 86). That long silence of the past is now broken as Namjoshi narrates her own life to Goja and Goldie.

A note on the dialogic structure of Namjoshi's autobiography is in order here: Goja and Goldie who are located as narratees initially do not remain silent listeners; in fact Namjoshi does not intend them to be mere audience, she expects them to be her auditors. They freely interrupt and intervene in the narration; contradict and cross-examine the narrator and at certain points take over the baton of narration to tell their tales in their own voices. This dialogic patterning establishes memory as a collective rather than a recollective faculty. Namjoshi and the two characters she conjures up indulge in arguments, discussions, mutual recrimination as well as appreciation. As Goja and Goldie appropriate the narrative authority from time to time and act as the auditors of the narrator, the reader grasps the important suggestion that there is nothing like ultimate truth or one authentic version of the past. Instead, there are perceptions which are at best tentative. Generally, an autobiographer is troubled by the fluidity of memory and the tentativeness of its recall. Namjoshi, on the other hand, enjoys the fluidity and provisionality of reconstituting selfhood and identities. Her own self in her autobiography is sinuous, shifting, vital and open to negotiation and even reflection on its own possibilities.

The last section titled 'Later' brings the narrative to the present, that is, Namjoshi's life in the UK as a writer, as an immigrant and as a lesbian. By now she has resolved most of her tensions in each of these roles. She has evolved a stable relationship with her companion, Gill Hanscombe, since both of them had understood that they had "to find something tougher and more lasting than just romantic love" (*Goja* 124). Here is a moment in lesbian love where the partners achieve a harmony of psychological as well as physical empathy. As an exile she has come to terms with the fact of racial discrimination. Referring to the British response to the Indian presence in England, she says: "They use us as a backdrop on which they were once able to strut. I don't like it, but I suppose it is understandable" (*Goja* 125). It is this capacity to historicize the present that enables one to perceive things in a proper perspective. As a writer too she has reached a point of self-revelation. She writes now to speak out, confess and make a clean breast of things concerning her past and her present.

Namjoshi, Goja and Goldie confide in each other, as they never did in reality. Goldie tells how difficult it was for her to play the matriarch all the time. If Goat is born into poverty and thralldom, Goldie claims that she too was born into the constraints of her role as the great and golden Ranisaheb placed on her. Namjoshi realizes that each one of them has found oneself in situations from which there was no escape: Goja as a servant in a world dominated by the rich, Goldie as the Ranisaheb of a royal family very much under the control of the British, Namjoshi as a lesbian in a predominantly heterosexual society. Three of them re-view their past and make assessments; examine the role each one played; defend their own positions; and finally ask each other's forgiveness. In this retrospective analysis it emerges that Goja still is the most unjustly exploited of them all, and it is not easy for the rich to find expiation for the sins they had committed against the poor. The whole point of writing this account is to seek forgiveness from Goja. Namjoshi is in quest for love and charity here and it is therefore important to seek these from Goldie and Goja. It was easy asking for her grandmother's forgiveness for having abandoned her and gone off to the West; but she cannot possibly tell Goja, "Forgive me that I exploited you, day in and day out, year after year" (*Goja* 144). Yet it is necessary for her survival to pray for Goja's charity. Interestingly, her first chapter is entitled 'Goja', and again her penultimate chapter is called 'What Goja Said'. To Namjoshi's insistent question as to whether or not Goja really loved her, the latter replies:

> Not much to be said. But you want to extract something? Very well, in all that morass there was some kinship and some kindness.
> I cannot, and may not say all is forgotten and forgiven. I will Not collude.
>
> (*Goja* 152)

Having thus found her peace, Namjoshi rows backwards, bidding farewell to her ancestors.

It is interesting to note Namjoshi's self-consciousness in this work about the nature of autobiographical act and the writing of fiction. In fact the relation between fiction and autobiography is the contentious focus of most critical theorizing about autobiographical writing and recent theory erases the tenuous borders once acknowledged. Much of what happens in Goja is reflective interaction of past and present, which of course is the active condition of all autobiographical writing. In this temporal dimension, the autobiographer's shaping vision is itself shaped by what Georges Gurdof has called "an unavoidable optical illusion", whereby "the act of reflection that is essential to conscious awareness is transferred back... to the stage of the event itself" (1980: 41). This is the active condition of all autobiographical discourse, eliding the gap between the facts of the past and the voice of the present in which those facts live, move and have their being. Autobiography is not curtailed by facts, which it transforms even as it brings them to life, as it gives life to them. The autobiographer too is in turn transformed by the whole exercise of recall, recapitulation, rehearsal and revelation. Namjoshi hopes to evoke a similar transformation in her readers too. She tells us: "If my quest makes you remember and praise what was valuable in your own life, then my task will have been done" ("Preface" *Goja* x). I am sure the time will prove that her task is not only done, but well done.

Works Cited

Frame, Janet. *An Angel at My Table*. 1984. London: Paladin, 1987.

Gusdorf, Georges. "Conditions and Limits of Autobiography" (1956). Trans. James Olney in *Autobiography: Essays Theoretical and Critical*. Ed. James Olney. Princeton: Princeton University Press, 1980.

Jay, Karla. "Coming Out as a Process", in *Our Right to Love: A Lesbian Resource Book*. Englewood Cliffs, New Jersey: Prentice Hall Inc, 1978. 28-30.

Maslow, A. *Motivation and Personality*. New York: Harper and Row, 1954.

Namjoshi, Suniti. *Goja: An Autobiographical Myth*. Melbourne, Australia: Spinifex, 2000.

Pollio, H.R. *Behaviour and Existence*. Monterey, C.A.: Brooks/Cole, 1982.

Warland, Betsy. *Proper Definitions: Collected Theorograms*. Vancouver: Gang Publishers, 1990.

Wisker, Gina. "Introduction: Black and White; Voices, Writers and Readers," in *Black Women's Writing*. Ed. Wisker. New York: St Martin's, 1993.

Zimmerman, Bonnie. "Exiting from Patriarchy: the Lesbian Novel of Development", in *The Voyage In: Fictions of Female Development*. Eds. Elizabeth Abel, Marianna Hirsch and Elizabeth Langland. Hanover: University Press of New England, 1983. 244-57.

Interview with Suniti Namjoshi

While working on this book, I had the opportunity to correspond with Suniti Namjoshi (on email) periodically, and she was kind enough to respond to my questions from time to time. My questions and her responses are included here (with the permission of the author) for the benefit of readers:

I will begin by asking you about some of your early work in print, translations of the poems of Govindagraj you have done with your mother and grandmother. Did this collaboration have a definitive impact on you as a writer and a person? How did your family influence your work?

My first book in print was *Poems* (Calcutta: Writers Workshop, 1967). The translation of the Poems of Govindagraj was done later and published a year later. I did these poems with my mother, Sarojini Namjoshi. Round about this time I also did a few translations of some of the poems of the great

Maratha *bhakti* poets, Eknath, Namdev and Tukaram. These I did with the help of my grandmother (Laxmi Devi Naik Nimbalkar) and my mother.

My mother is genuinely bilingual and can appreciate both Marathi literature and English literature. My grandmother's Marathi was superb. Her English was less good. For me it was the other way about. I was educated in English, and think in English. Though we spoke Marathi at home, I was never formally taught Marathi.

I was young and brash and in my early twenties when I undertook the translations. Had I understood the difficulties more clearly, I don't think I'd have undertaken the work so lightheartedly or done it so superficially. In spite of that, trying to do the work did make me begin to understand the need to struggle with language in order to make it more malleable, in order somehow to make it express an alien sensibility.

I was mostly brought up by my mother's family. My father died when his plane crashed in 1953. At the time he was the test pilot at Hindustan Aircraft, Bangalore. My mother's family was a traditional, liberal Hindu family. I loved and respected the family, particularly my grandmother. The existence of the family was a source of tremendous support and strength, but the very strength of the ties also made it extremely difficult to rebel against them.

What are the early formative influences on your work?

The two central influences were the fact of growing up in India, and the fact of thinking in English. I was sent to an American boarding school in Mussoorie, and then to a school in the south run on J. Krishnamurthi's principles for a year or so. The Indian cultural context is extraordinarily dense, but the language one thinks in also carries with it the weight of a strong cultural tradition (and in this case a different tradition).

In your introduction to the Jackass section in *Because of India* you talked about "not entirely happy confluence of western and Hindu influences in your work." Could you tell me more about this cultural conflict/confluence in your creative work?

I've looked up the passage referred to. (Remember I wrote it ten years ago, and it refers in turn to a time earlier than that.) I'm not entirely sure what I meant. I don't think I'm referring to a cultural conflict, but rather to the use I made of the Hindu notion that there was not a clear cut division between human being and animals in order to deal with my alienation from the male-centred Western humanist tradition. This is too polysyllabic. I think all I meant was that if to be centrally human meant that one had to be an Anglo Saxon heterosexual male, then I personally would rather identify with the birds and the beasts. I suppose this was an "unhappy" choice because it accepted marginalization. A "happier" choice, which I made later, was to claim centre stage for the dispossessed and to challenge the traditional assumptions.

You have often rewritten tales of female characters from western classical literature -- Eurydice, Medusa, Circe and so on. But never tried to resurrect the heroines of *The Ramayana* or *The Mahabharata*. I wonder why.

I think it's probably because I'm simply not well versed enough in the Sanskrit and (later the Marathi) literary tradition. I have used some Hindu references here and there. But just to know a story isn't enough. In order to subvert established assumptions, reveal surprising connections, make certain juxtapositions, and allow multiple ironies to make a pattern, one needs a fairly thorough understanding of the language and of the tradition. Perhaps the images one uses also has to do with what sparks one's imagination -- with the words and the books and the images that one's head is filled with.

I feel that *The Authentic Lie* is the most serious and the saddest of all your work. Were you going through some emotional turmoil at the time of writing these verses?

No. On the contrary I was able to write *The Authentic Lie*, because at last I felt strong enough to be able to deal with the material and also because I had learnt more of my craft. I've said earlier that my father was killed when his plane crashed. This happened before I could see him. I was twelve at the time. When I had last seen him I had been eleven. Anyhow the result was a recurrent dream which troubled me year after year. In the dream my father wasn't dead, he had only been lost, but now he had come back. What was terrible was waking up and realising it wasn't true. The dream altered subtly over the years. I think I must have written "Discourse with the Dead" in 1979 or so. It took a long time to come to terms with my father's death and to be able to write about it. (*The Authentic Lie* was written before *Feminist Fables* though it was published later.)

There is a marked change in the tone of your writing beginning with *The Conversations of Cow*. There is a greater playfulness and detachment. Would you agree with this view?

No, not entirely. *Feminist Fables*, for example, is perhaps at least as literary and playful as it is feminist. And it's worth considering that feminism in its broadest sense questions the roles the powerful assign to themselves in relation to the relatively powerless.

Tell me Sunitiji, how did you conjure up that fabulous creature – Blue Donkey?

It was Gill's birthday and I had bought her a birthday card with Marc Chagall's picture of the blue donkey on it. I thought I ought to write a fable to go with it and so wrote the first blue donkey fable. At the time I had submitted a manuscript consisting mostly of poems to Ros de Lanerolle of The Women's Press. (I was naïve then.) She explained to me that it would have to be filled out with more fables – more prose. And so I wrote the rest of the blue donkey fables in the book. Sometimes a particular image or a creature fires one's imagination and then what needs to be said more or less says itself.

There are three sets of fables in your work – *Feminist Fables, Blue Donkey Fables* and *Solidarity Fables*. The first is primarily concerned with making feminist statements, the second quite witty and delightful, the third a little enigmatic. Your more recent work seems to be getting more enigmatic – Is that right?

In *Feminist Fables* I wasn't so much concerned with making feminist statements as with using the form to understand the imbalance of power and to question it. In *The Blue Donkey Fables* I had applied myself to literary form again. Many of the fables and poems are concerned with poetry – how it works, what it does and might do. The "Solidarity" fables were simply added to the *Saint Suniti and the Dragon* manuscript because Virago wanted a thicker volume. By that time the lack of solidarity within the feminist movement had manifested itself and the word is used with a degree of irony. They're a more disparate lot.

It's nice of you to use the word "enigmatic" rather than "obscure". I don't want to be enigmatic or obscure. I think that it's just that the themes I'm tackling in my later work are more difficult. I don't want to write the same old book or repeat the same old forms mechanically. I have never tried deliberately to create new forms or to be innovative for the sake of innovation. I've just used whatever means seemed necessary for my purpose.

Could you please tell me something about the background to your St Suniti? Canonization of Suniti and her encounter with the Dragon –

Saint Suniti is concerned with the problem of trying to be a good person. It works on three levels: the internal or psychological level, where what is feared are monsters of one's own making; the day to day level, where though one would like to be nice (good), it's too hard because too much is required of one; and the wider historical and political level where dreadful things happen, but where taking effective action seems hopeless or impossible. S is three people -- the name on the cover of the book, the writer within the work, and the unheroic protagonist at the centre of the work. Saint S fails in her saintly aspirations, but the result is not the victory of evil over good. As depicted here evil isn't something magnificent, it's just a failure to grow up -- it means continuing to be frightened by internal monsters and devils.

***Building Babel* is an experimental text both in terms of its intent and narrative. It incorporates several contemporary critical/theoretical assumptions and practices such as notions of identity and culture, practices of reading and interpretation, the role of reader etc. Would you like to share with me your experiences in writing this unusual book?**

I had set myself a task---not out of vainglory---but because I wanted to do the best work that I could. *Saint Suniti* was my *Inferno. Building Babel* was, if I might say so, my *Purgatorio*. Its central theme is the process of building culture under the aegis of Crone Kronos, i.e. subject to time. Since culture is built out of other bits of culture, I had to show this process in the work---I had to embody the process. The characters themselves then become bits of culture which mutate. Handing over the final chapter to the Reader is in keeping with the central theme. By making more poems and stories out of the bits and pieces of this story, the cultural process is continued. Cyberspace is only a particular form of the common cultural space we have always had. It's not the links between computers that matter, but the links between human brains. The internet forms a perfect analogue to the cultural process. That is why I have used it. And I've used the concept of *memes*, because it's a handy way to refer to bits of culture. But I haven't consciously incorporated or critiqued contemporary critical theory. I'm not well versed in it. I belong to the generation for whom the study of literature meant reading poetry.

Generally, expatriate writing shows an insistent preoccupation with themes of alienation, rootlessness, nostalgia for home, creating imaginary homelands and so on. You too talk about these things, but you seem to have found a way of coping with these experiences. What kind of impact has living in different countries, climates and cultural milieus had on your writing?

It may be that *Goja*, which I describe as "An Autobiographical Myth", and which is to be published by Spinifex Press next year, will answer or at least help with many of the questions you've asked. (Goja is the name of the woman who looked after me when I was little.) There's one passage from *Goja* that might be relevant here:

> Now, as I try to put together the two halves of my experience, I live in the country in England with my partner. This, once again, is an entirely different landscape – sometimes it's like living inside an emerald. If I had told Goja and my grandmother all those years ago that I did not mean to return, it would not have been true. I have returned year after year for the past thirty years. And then I have returned again and again year after year to the West like some silly goose or determined salmon. In the course of those years both Goja and my grandmother have died. I did not mean to abandon them. I could not.

I had thought once that I felt most at home in a plane in mid-air; but that isn't true. I belong to India and to the West. Both belong to me and both reject me. I have to make sense of what has been and what there is.

In *Goja*, which you'll have guessed is supposed to correspond to the *Paradiso*, I try to celebrate Love or Charity. I also try to bridge the polarities, which have formed so much of my experience -- between the east and the west, the past and the present, the rich and the poor.

Now coming to the question of lesbianism – would you consider it a possible sexual alternative or an important feminist concern? Again there is a point of view that Lesbianism is a Western phenomenon, does culture have something to do with one's sexual choices?

It is and was an important feminist concern because of the intersection of power with sexuality, because of sexual politics, because of the ways in which heterosexual institutions work to maintain the *status quo*. In my opinion the willingness to hurt, hate and damage other people is a moral issue, not sexual orientation. Homophobia, racism and sexism are all ways of putting people down in order to exercise control over them, perhaps get at their property, deprive them of jobs, force them to conform and so forth. The people who say lesbians are only found in the West presumably think that homosexuality is something to be ashamed of. I think that the fact that we still haven't got rid of Section 377 of the Indian Penal Code – I think that's the one that makes homosexuality a crime – is far more shameful. Yes, culture has a great deal to do with one's sexual choices, and indeed with the formation of one's very identity. That's precisely why cultural assumptions can be questioned. Conservative forces are by definition in favour of maintaining the *status quo*, i.e. of ensuring that those in power stay in power and those who are relatively powerless remain so.

In short, I don't believe sexuality is a matter of "nature", or of "morality". It's the meanings and symbolism attributed to sexuality that are crucial, and when analysed it's clear that many of these are are inimical to women – all women, not just lesbians.

Could you tell me something about your current projects –?

I've told you something about *Goja*. With its completion I feel I've done what I set out to do to the best of my ability; and I feel glad to have been given the chance. I don't mean I'm not allowed to write any more, just that I no longer have to drive myself.

Bibliography

Primary

Books by Namjoshi

Poems. Calcutta: Writers Workshop, 1967.

Poems of Govindagraj. Calcutta: Writers Workshop, 1968. Translated from the Marathi with Sarojini Namjoshi.

More Poems. Calcutta: Writers Workshop, 1971.

Cyclone in Pakistan. Calcutta: Writers Workshop, 1971.

The Jackass and the Lady. Calcutta: Writers Workshop, 1980.

Feminist Fables. London: Sheba Feminist Publishers, 1981.

The Authentic Lie. Frederiction, Canada: Fiddlehead, 1982.

From the Bedside Book of Nightmares. Frederiction, Canada: Fiddlehead, 1984.

The Conversations of Cow. London: The Women's Press, 1985.

Aditi and the One-eyed Monkey. London: Sheba, 1986. Children's Book.

Flesh and Paper with Gillian Hanscombe. U.K.: Jezebel Tapes and Books, 1986.

The Blue Donkey Fables. London: The Women's Press, 1988.

The Mothers of Maya Diip. London: The Women's Press, 1989.

Because of India: Selected Poems. London: Onlywomen Press, 1989.

Saint Suniti and the Dragon. Melbourne: Spinifex, 1993; London: Virago, 1994.

*Building Babe*l. Melbourne: Spinifex Press, 1996.

Goja. Melbourne: Spinifex Press, 2000.

Plays

Kaliyug: Circles of Paradise with Gillian Hanscombe for Pan Project, first performed 1993.

Papers

Manuscripts, other material and Personal Papers are located in the Thomas Fisher Rare Book Library, University of Toronto.

Secondary

Selected Namjoshi Criticism

Acharya, Gayatri. "Soaring on the Wings of Fabulist Imagination." Review of *Feminist Fables, Saint Suniti and the Dragon*. *The Book Review* 20. 2-3, (Feb-Mar 1996): 53-54.

Banerji, Jaya. "Slaying the Male Dragon". Review of *Feminist Fables* and *Saint Suniti and the Dragon*. *Indian Review of Books* 5.3 (Jan-Feb 1996): 31.

Chavan, Sunanda P. "The New Poets I: Mamta Kalia, Suniti Namjoshi, Gauri Deshpande." *The Fair Voice: A Study of Indian Women Poets in English*. Ed. Chavan Sunanda P. New Delhi: Sterling Publishers, 1984: 72-83.

Dwivedi, A. N. "Suniti Namjoshi—Art and Artifice in Her Work." *Studies in Contemporary Indo-English Verse* Vol: 1. Bareilly: Prakash Book Depot, 1984: 227-239.

Jain, Jasbir. "Suniti Namjoshi: The Dual World of Her Early Poems." *Problems of Postcolonial Literatures and Other Essays*. Ed. Jain Jasbir. Jaipur: Printwell Publishers, 1991. 109-120.

Kathleen Jamie, "Female-Centred Fables." *Times Literary Supplement*, 14 Sept. 1990.

Lakshmi Kannan, "Fables for the Future." *The Times of India*. 18 Dec. 1988.

Lane, M. Travis. "I and My Creature: Three Versions of the Human." *Fiddlehead* 145 (Autumn 1985): 94-100.

Mann, Harveen Sachdeva. " 'Cracking India': Minority Women Writers and the Contentious Margins of Indian Nationalist Discourse." *The Journal of Commonwealth Literature* 29.2 (1994): 71-94.

McGifford, Diane. "Suniti Namjoshi (1941-)," *Writers of the Indian Diaspora: A Bio-Bibliographical Critical Source Book*. Ed. Nelson Emmanuel S. Connecticut: Greenwood Press, 1993: 291-297.

Parameswaran, Uma. "Literature of the Indian Diaspora in Canada." *Commonwealth Literature: Themes and Techniques*. Ed. Rajan P.K., et al.; Delhi: Ajanta Publishers, 1993: 102-125.

Paranjape, Makarand. "New Fiction by Expatriate Indian Women". *World Literature Today* 65.1, (Winter 1991): 72-80.

Raja, P. Review of *The Jackass and the Lady*. *The Literary Endeavour*, 2.4, 55-56.

Reuben, E. Review of *Cycone in Pakistan*. *The Indian P.E.N.* 38.4 (Apr 1972): 101-103.

Sawton, Ian. "Pastoral Lines." *Canadian Literature* 97 (Summer 1983): 124-126.

Seshadri, Veena. "She is No Silly Cow." *Indian Review of Books* 3.3 (Dec-Jan 1994): 36.

Simon, Sherry. "Review of *The Jackass and the Lady, The Authentic Lie, Feminist Fables*" *The Literary Criterion* 20.1 (1985): 261-267.

Varma, Monika. "Suniti Namjoshi", *Facing Four*. Calcutta: Writers Workshop Publication, 1973: 3-11.

Vijayasree, C. "Alter-Nativity, Migration, Marginality and Narration: The Case of Indian Women Writers Settled in the West", *Shifting Continents/Colliding Cultures*. Ed. Ralph. J. Crane and Radhika Mohanram. Amsterdam: Rodopi, 2000. 123-135.

York, Lorraine. "Monsters Within." *Canadian Literature* 105 (Summer 1985): 190-92.

Index